Risa Brooks

Political–Military Relations and the Stability of Arab Regimes

Adelphi Paper 324

Oxford University Press, Great Clarendon Street, Oxford OX2 6DP
Oxford New York
Athens Auckland Bangkok Bombay Calcutta Cape Town
Dar es Salaam Delhi Florence Hong Kong Istanbul Karachi
Kuala Lumpur Madras Madrid Melbourne Mexico City
Nairobi Paris Singapore Taipei Tokyo Toronto
and associated companies in
Berlin Ibadan

Oxford is a trade mark of Oxford University Press

Published in the United States
by Oxford University Press Inc., New York

© International Institute for Strategic Studies 1998

First published December 1998 by **Oxford University Press** for
International Institute for Strategic Studies
23 Tavistock Street, London WC2E 7NQ

Director John Chipman
Editor Gerald Segal
Assistant Editor Matthew Foley
Design and Production Mark Taylor

British Library Cataloguing in Publication Data
Data available

Library of Congress Cataloguing in Publication Data

ISBN 0-19-922420-X
ISSN 0567-932X

contents

tables

glossary

AOI	Arab Organisation for Industrialisation
CPF	Central Protection Force (Egypt)
EDA	Excess Defense Articles (US)
FIS	*Front Islamique de Salut*
FMF	Foreign Military Financing (US)
GDP	gross domestic product
IAF	Islamic Action Front
IMF	International Monetary Fund
MB	Muslim Brotherhood
PA	Palestinian Authority
PLO	Palestine Liberation Organisation

introduction

By contemporary standards, the longevity of many Arab regimes is striking. One of the region's most resilient leaders, Jordan's King Hussein, acceded to the throne in 1953; Hafez al-Assad assumed the Syrian presidency in 1970; Hosni Mubarak took control in Egypt in 1981; and Saddam Hussein became Iraq's official head of state in 1979. After decades of rule, these leaders are among the Arab world's most enduring figures. This durability is all the more remarkable given the turbulence that marked most Arab states' early years of independence. Nearly every Arab regime endured at least one, and often many, serious attempts at a military takeover in the aftermath of the Second World War.[1]

Although coups have become less frequent, the military remains a key force in most Arab regimes. Maintaining its loyalty is essential to retaining office, and regimes have used a range of methods to ensure its backing, or at least its acquiescence. These include increasing non-military support by cultivating social, economic and religious groups; courting the high command and officer corps with corporate and private benefits; appointing members of specific groups – often privileged minorities – to key posts in the armed forces; and preventing officers from building a support-base within the military by purging potential opponents, monitoring military activity, rotating commands and establishing independent security services reporting directly to the presidency or the palace. Filling the military with religious or tribal minorities has been crucial to maintaining control over the armed forces in Iraq, Jordan and Syria. In Egypt, the military's substantial participation in military and non-military production has helped to give it a vested interest in the status quo. In Syria, Assad inherited a regime purged of competing religious, ethnic and ideological factions in the military and *Ba'ath* Party. He has since prevented the growth of new challengers in the armed forces by exploiting selective appointments, relying on privileged minorities and establishing security agencies operating outside the formal military chain of command. King Hussein has ensured that key positions in the armed forces are held by native East Bank Jordanians, whose support is the bedrock of his regime.

Despite the wealth of studies on Arab regimes and the many assessments of their military capabilities, there is a dearth of analysis of political–military relations in the Middle East.[2] This paper argues that the political–military balance is at the core of these regimes' politics. The need for Arab regimes to maintain political control over their armed forces raises two important but under-appreciated issues:

- first, the methods used often undermine the combat potential of the armed forces; and
- second, the fact that regimes have successfully managed political–military relations in the past does not mean that they will automatically do so in the future. Regime stability cannot therefore be taken for granted.

Leadership stability has come at the expense of conventional military capabilities. Arab armies have rarely realised their potential on the battlefield, in part because the methods regimes use to ensure their loyalty often conflict with the principles of efficient military organisation. Centralising command structures, politicising appointments, authorising economic activity, buying prestige equipment rather than essential, but less glamorous, items, and exploiting sectarianism and tribalism have all limited the military capabilities of Arab armed forces.

This paper examines the origins and implications of leadership stability in Arab regimes, primarily Egypt, Jordan and Syria.[3]

These states are pivotal to the region because of their geographical, political and historical importance. They are also frequently singled out as examples of firmly entrenched political control over the military. How this control is maintained, and whether it will persist, is therefore particularly important. Turbulent periods in political–military relations – in Jordan in the 1950s; in Egypt in the 1960s; in Syria in the late 1970s and early 1980s; and in Iraq since the late 1980s – suggest that political–military relations could again deteriorate should social and political conditions change. Simmering social discontent over the unevenly distributed benefits of economic reform in Egypt, together with growing unhappiness in Jordan over the illusory 'peace dividend' of the 1994 treaty with Israel, could upset the delicate political–military balance in these regimes. Syria, Jordan, Libya and the Palestinian Authority (PA) are all ruled by ageing or ill leaders; Iraq by a regime facing potential widespread social opposition; and Egypt by a President with no clear successor. Mubarak's near-assassination in Addis Ababa in 1995 is a grim reminder of the possibility of the untimely death of any of these leaders.

Leadership succession presents a particular challenge to the political–military balance: relations between aspiring leaders and their armed forces will dictate how these transitions unfold. The ability of new leaders to gain and maintain social support, to appoint allies to key posts, to marginalise competing factions and to attend to the military's corporate welfare and its officers' private interests will be crucial to the consolidation of power.

chapter 1

The Stability of Arab Regimes

The first wave of military coups in the Middle East coincided with the independence of most Arab states after the Second World War.[1] In 1949, just three years after independence, Syria experienced three coups in rapid succession; until Assad took power in 1970, the country endured 14 serious attempts at a military takeover. In 1952, the monarchy was ousted in Egypt; a similar fate befell the Hashemites in Iraq six years later. Between 1961 and 1969, according to analyst Eliezer Be'eri, 27 coups and attempted coups took place in nine Arab countries. As Be'eri puts it, 'the continuous interference and the ascendance of army officers in the political life of their countries is the most specific feature of Arab history in this era'.[2]

By contrast, successful military coups have become virtually non-existent since the late 1970s. Political–military relations have been relatively calm and regional leaderships stable. Coup plots have persisted, but have rarely been executed; they have generally been snuffed out through 'back-door' arrests, rather than put down by loyalist units on the streets of the region's capitals. Even in Iraq, where reports of arrests and subsequent purges are frequent, coup attempts rarely reach the point where men take up arms.

King Hussein, Mubarak and Assad have all proven adept at managing their relations with their militaries. King Hussein formally acceded to the Jordanian throne in 1953 following the assassination of his grandfather, King Abdullah, in 1951 and the abdication of his father, King Talal, in 1952. After dismissing the

Table 1 *Arab Heads of State*

Country	Head of State	Accession
Algeria	President Liamine Zéroual	*January 1994; elected, November 1995*
Bahrain	Emir Sheikh Isa bin Sulman al-Khalifa	*Succeeded to the throne, 1961; took title of Emir, 1971*
Egypt	President Hosni Mubarak	*October 1981*
Iraq	President Saddam Hussein	*July 1979*
Jordan	King Hussein I	*May 1953*
Kuwait	Emir Sheikh Jabir al-Ahmad al-Jabir al-Sabah	*Chosen from among Royal Family, December 1977*
Lebanon	President General Emile Lahoud	*Elected by parliament, October 1998*
Libya	Col Muammar Gaddafi	*'Leader of the Revolution' since military coup, September 1969*
Morocco	King Hassan II	*March 1961*
Oman	Sultan Qaboos bin Said al-Said	*July 1970*
Qatar	Emir Sheikh Hamad bin Khalifa al-Thani	*'Palace coup', June 1995*
Saudi Arabia	King Fahd ibn Abdul Aziz al Saud	*June 1982*
Syria	President Hafez al-Assad	*November 1970*
Tunisia	President Zein al-Abdin Ben Ali	*November 1987*
UAE	President Sheikh Zayed bin Sultan al-Nahyan	*Elected by Supreme Council, December 1971*
Yemen	President Ali Abdullah Saleh	*Elected by House of Representatives, May 1990*

Arab Legion's British commander, General Sir John Glubb, in 1956, King Hussein began to 'Arabise' the country's army, appointing native-Jordanian officers to principal commands. The bulk of the armed forces comprise members of the East Bank Jordanian tribes (also commonly referred to as Transjordanians or Bedouin).[3] King Hussein appears to have gained the upper hand over his armed forces early in his rule. He weathered a strong challenge in 1957 from leftist officers led by the pro-republican army commander Ali Abu Nuwar, as well as a wave of coup attempts backed by Egypt and Syria. A decade later, the King faced a military apprehensive about his decision to form a military pact with Egypt and enter the 1967 Arab–Israeli War. In the turbulence leading to the suppression of Palestinian militants in 1970, King Hussein faced military opposition over his reluctance to sanction a crackdown. When he finally ordered the militants' violent suppression – the regime's 'Black September' – the military firmly backed him. None of these events led to widespread military defiance, and King Hussein survived to celebrate his forty-fifth year in power on 2 May 1998.

Aside from the hereditary monarchies, Egypt is one of the few Arab states to have transferred power without a coup – from Gamal Abdel Nasser to Anwar Sadat in 1970, and from Sadat to Mubarak in 1981. Nonetheless, since the July 1952 coup against King Farouk that brought the Free Officers to power, there have been episodes of military dissent and the discovery of nascent coup groupings. In the 1960s, Nasser faced a challenge from the military under Field Marshal Abdel Hakim Amer; the balance of political power shifted in Amer's favour, culminating in what was later reported as an abortive coup attempt in 1967 following the war with Israel. Sadat reportedly pre-empted a coup attempt when he ousted his leftist opponents in 1971. The most strident domestic challenge since the 1970s has come from militant Islamists, who reject Egypt's secular regime and seek to establish a state based on Islamic principles. Although there are suspicions that fundamentalist elements in the military participated in Sadat's assassination in 1981, these groups generally operate outside the state's formal structures. They thus pose a primarily indirect threat. Internal disunity has handicapped their effectiveness, and their violent tactics have alienated potential supporters. However, if militants garner sufficient popular support, they could lay the groundwork for a military-backed movement against the government. That they have failed to provoke a movement of this kind testifies in part to Mubarak's effective management of relations with the armed forces.

Assad's accession in Syria in 1970 marked the end of a series of coups and counter-coups since independence in 1946. Initially, these rebellions were fuelled by clashes between competing sectarian and class interests as civilian groups joined forces with factions in the military. By the 1960s, however, coup-making had become enmeshed with the intrigues of *Ba'ath* Party politics as factions of the Party élite competed for dominance, while Sunni Muslims and other minorities in the political apparatus and military were purged. After 1966, a power-struggle developed between Assad and his chief competitor within the Party, Salah Jadid; by early 1969, Assad had marginalised Jadid and his supporters and, in November 1970, seized power. Years of political infighting and the steady attrition of minority groups meant that sectarian and ideological factionalism were greatly reduced, both in Assad's regime and in the military.

The elimination of competing factions in the military has been crucial to Assad's ability to maintain power. There have nonetheless been turbulent periods in political–military relations. Syria's intervention in the Lebanese civil war in the mid-1970s, in particular the decision to turn against the Palestine Liberation Organisation (PLO), caused friction with some elements of the military, which saw it as a betrayal of the Palestinian cause. During the regime's lengthy battle with the Islamist Muslim Brotherhood (MB), which culminated in a bloody confrontation in Hama in 1982, there were reports that soldiers had deserted or joined the insurgents, presumably out of disillusion with the mass repression, or because of sympathy with the rebels.[4] Nevertheless, the bulk of the forces remained loyal to the regime.

Arguably the strongest challenge faced by Assad's regime has come from his brother Rifaat, whose Defence Companies, a 35,000–55,000-strong unit of the armed forces, played an important role in the suppression of Islamist opposition in the late 1970s and 1980s. Rifaat's part in crushing the Hama uprising and his command of the Defence Companies increased his already substantial influence, allowing him to pursue his own foreign and domestic policies, even when they were at odds with those of the regime. When in late 1983 Assad fell seriously ill, Rifaat organised a bid for power, leading to a three-month stand-off on the streets of Damascus until, in May 1984, Rifaat was sidelined. The Defence Companies were stripped of their formal title and high profile in regime security.[5] Despite periodic arrests and murmurs of coup plotting, Assad has maintained a firm grip on the military since coming to power.

Coups have become less frequent in the Arab world. Nonetheless, although its public role differs over time and between regimes, the military remains a pivotal constituency in most Arab states. The Egyptian military shed its ideological trappings after the *débâcle* of the 1967 war, but was initially a prominent symbol of the regime; as the 'vanguard of the revolution', the armed forces were closely identified with Nasser's domestic and international policies. The military's symbolic resonance has been less marked both in Jordan, where the regime tends to be associated more with King Hussein and the Hashemite monarchy, and in the hereditary monarchies of the

fewer coups, but a still-pivotal military

Gulf states. These distinctions notwithstanding, maintaining the military's loyalty is essential to retaining office in the Arab world's authoritarian regimes. As Be'eri puts it: 'Without the active participation or at least the expressive approval of commanders of the military, no Arab government can hold on to the reigns of power'.[6]

Although the degree of political liberalisation varies between states, no Arab regime is truly democratic; coercion, not consent, is the basis of political order. Although Egypt is known for its wide circulation of periodicals, Mubarak's sustained clampdown on his country's press illustrates the limits of political expression there.[7] Despite democratic reforms in the late 1980s, Jordan's electoral system has yet to become truly representative. Parliamentary elections in November 1997, for example, favoured the native East Bank tribes, whose position was further bolstered by the opposition's decision in 1993 to boycott the polls in protest at electoral reforms which strengthened tribal linkages at the expense of political parties. Human-rights organisations regularly cite Syria for its repression of personal and political freedoms.[8] Generally, regimes sharply circumscribe parliamentary debate and decision-making; opposition is constrained and representation limited, with parliaments acting as outlets for decisions taken behind closed doors.

The military's central position stems from its status as the primary repository of force, and hence the final guarantor of power. In Egypt in 1986, the Interior Ministry failed to suppress a 15,000–20,000-strong riot by its Central Protection Force (CPF). The unrest was only quelled following the deployment of three divisions – about a quarter of the regular army – and air force helicopters.[9] Similarly, when Rifaat made his bid for power in 1984, Special Forces and other loyal military units came to the regime's rescue. The Jordanian military was called in after the police failed to suppress riots at Karak in 1996; two years later, the military again played a prominent role in restoring order after riots in the southern city of Ma'an.[10] The dependence of leaders on their militaries means that maintaining the political backing of the armed forces is essential to staying in power. Like any pivotal constituency, the military's support must be cultivated, and its opposition guarded against.

chapter 2

Maintaining Power

Ensuring political control over the military entails depriving it of both the means and the motives to challenge the regime.[1] Leaders use a combination of inducements and safeguards to give the armed forces a vested interest in the status quo, and to make it difficult for them to conspire against the regime by increasing the costs and risks of doing so. Some measures are broad and difficult to implement, such as cultivating non-military support. Others are more specific and straightforward, including rotating commands or centralising the chain of command. The methods used vary from regime to regime but, in general, political leaders establish and maintain control of their armed forces in four main ways.

- First, they try to increase non-military support by cultivating social, economic and religious groups. This tends to reduce the regime's reliance on the armed forces, thereby lessening their political influence.[2]
- Second, they court the high command and officer corps with corporate and private benefits, thereby 'buying' their complicity.
- Third, they appoint members of specific groups to key posts. These groups are often privileged minorities that are also well-represented within the regime itself, thereby ensuring that the preferences of the officer corps coincide with those of the political leadership.

- Fourth, they use various tactics, from frequent posting rotations to extensive monitoring and purges, to prevent ambitious challengers from establishing an independent power-base, and to make it more difficult to organise and execute a military takeover.[3] Thus, the regime guards against opportunism from within the high command, and also against conspiracies from the lower ranks.

Expanding a Regime's Social Base

In its most diffuse and all-encompassing form, political control over the military is sustained by cultivating social support *outside* the armed forces, among core groups that underpin the regime and within society at large. Economic interests, religious minorities, tribal and clan groups, party apparatuses, popular or mass support and even the backing of international agencies and governments can be significant elements in the social infrastructure of Arab regimes. In effect, civilian backing counter-balances the military, much as the absence of this support, or the presence of outright opposition, increases a regime's dependence on force and strengthens the political influence of the armed forces.

In Egypt, popular disillusionment with Farouk's dissipated and corrupt regime nurtured the Free Officers' movement and helped make possible the military coup that ousted the monarchy in July 1952. Similarly, Syria's short-lived pre-Assad regimes proved incapable of establishing a social base or winning popular support. By contrast, soon after taking power in 1970 Assad undertook limited reforms that increased popular backing for his regime, helping him to consolidate his position. He relaxed many of his predecessors' oppressive policies, promised to restore limited civil liberties and to establish a parliament (although not a democracy), and pledged the 'development [that is, relaxation] of socialism'.[4] Although many of these gestures were more symbolic than substantive, Assad eased the virtual reign of terror that had dominated public life. The repeal of his predecessors' most severe socialist policies led to a surge in economic growth which appeased the urban middle classes: 'Asad's shrewd alliance with the Damascene bourgeoisie significantly changed the regime's complexion and won it new, tentative legitimacy among crucial sectors of the population'.[5]

Assad also sought to secure his rule by cultivating the Alawi religious minority, from which he originates.[6] Under Assad, Alawis have occupied the key positions in the regime, colonising the military, the bureaucracy and other parts of the state apparatus.[7] However, Syrian society is a complex mix of ethnic and religious groups: while 10–12% are Alawi, some 74% are Sunni Muslim; Druze and other Muslim sects account for 6% and Christians approximately 10%. Assad has accordingly tried to expand the regime's social base beyond its Alawi core. Sunni Muslims have been well-represented in the regime, as have the country's religious minorities.[8] Sunnis, many of rural descent, account for around 60% of the membership of the People's Assembly, and of the *Ba'ath* Party Congresses. They have also traditionally held many of the regime's most public and outwardly influential posts. Foreign Minister Farouq al-Shara, Defence Minister Lieutenant-General Mustafa Tlas, Vice-President Abdel Halim Khaddam and former Chief of Staff Hikmat Shehabi, for example, are all Sunni.[9]

The growth of commercial interests prompted by economic liberalisation has added a new dimension to the regime's social fabric. Investment Law Number 10, announced in May 1991, encouraged private investment in the economy and gave fresh impetus to Syria's middle classes and commercial interests, many of whom *the economic basis* are of Sunni origin.[10] These measures *of regime support* broaden the regime's social bases, and shift its centre of gravity away from the military.[11] At the same time, Assad has controlled the pace of liberalisation; the networks of public-sector, military and *Ba'ath* Party officials appear intact.[12] Relations between large-scale private capital and these more traditional interests appear collaborative, although this could change, especially if private interests begin to press for political reforms that impinge on the prerogatives of the security and military chiefs.[13]

Economic interests also play an important role in shaping political–military relations in Egypt. Nasser's nationalisation of private industry and the financial sector in the early 1960s weakened the influence of private capital in the regime. Subsequent reforms introduced by Nasser following the 1967 war, and expanded by Sadat in the early 1970s, reinvigorated Egypt's urban capitalists.

Sadat also increased social support by encouraging greater personal and political freedom of expression, principles enshrined in the 1971 Constitution. Sadat's important 'October speech' of 1974 signalled the expansion of his *infitah* ('open door') policy and the growth of new financial and commercial interests.[14] Paradoxically, privatisation also coincided with increased public-sector and civil-service employment, which had already grown dramatically under Nasser. Between 1975 and 1978, the regime added over four million employees to the public payroll.[15] At the same time, the armed forces' political influence suffered an unprecedented decline. After coming to power, Sadat also made overtures to the Islamist interests that Nasser had suppressed. By the late 1970s, however, he faced an increasingly militant Islamist opposition, demonstrating the difficulties inherent in trying to expand social support through liberalisation, while maintaining a firm grip on the activities of newly mobilised groups. Growing anti-government sentiment and increasing social turmoil, notably severe rioting in 1977 prompted by proposals to remove food subsidies, strengthened the political influence and the resources of the security forces and the conventional armed forces.[16]

When Mubarak came to power in 1981, he inherited his predecessors' contradictory policies and a social base that reflected them: a resurgent semi-aristocracy; a so-called 'state bourgeoisie' that had evolved from the mass nationalisation of the 1960s; and the financial and commercial classes encouraged by *infitah*.[17] Since the late 1980s, controlled economic liberalisation under an International Monetary Fund (IMF)-sponsored programme has stabilised the economy and created a climate in which middle-class business interests are prospering.[18] The onset of structural reforms, including the privatisation of major industries, should further invigorate private capital, thereby strengthening the regime's middle-class underpinnings. At the same time, Mubarak has preserved the social contract established by Nasser and perpetuated by Sadat by subsidising food and basic resources in exchange for popular complicity in the regime. He has also maintained a bloated public sector and bureaucracy, in which one in 11 Egyptians (over 5.4m people) is employed.[19] In general terms, these groups are the civilian bulwark of the regime.

The expansion of the private sector and of the middle class has important implications for the military's position in the regime. In the 1980s, the private sector coexisted and often collaborated with the military which, under then Defence Minister Field Marshal Abdel al-Halim Abu Ghazala, significantly expanded its economic activities.[20] However, the reforms of the 1990s and their attendant social changes may threaten the military's prerogatives.[21] Mubarak may be calculating that the gains from economic liberalisation may help him to withstand potential resistance from the armed forces. In March 1998, inflation stood at a low of 4% and the budget deficit was negligible.

threats to the military from economic reform

Between 1996 and mid-1997, real growth in gross domestic product (GDP) hovered around 5%.[22] If the benefits of moderate, steady economic expansion reach the mass of the population, popular support for the regime could rise, and the appeal of Islamist militancy fall, thereby allowing Mubarak to distance himself from the security apparatus.[23] Lifting the many restrictions on public life, including press laws, sanctions on professional associations and intrusive security measures, might win the regime further social acceptance. This would provide the basis for political liberalisation – even democratisation – and a more permanent military retreat from politics. However, investors' wariness of the regime's lack of transparency, corruption and arbitrary exercise of power in the short term may obstruct the investment and growth that could lead to political opening in the long term.[24]

In Jordan, King Hussein has exploited state-employment opportunities to establish a class of salaried workers dependent on the regime for their livelihoods. Although avowedly a free-market economy, the public sector accounts for nearly 50% of the country's employment, with some 150,000 working in the civil service and a similar number in the military.[25] Public-sector positions are reserved for native East Bankers, the bedrock of the regime. King Hussein has thus maintained a social consensus in favour of his rule. In short,

> *Employment in the bureaucracy and the perquisites that attend it have, especially since the early 1970s, been an important form of distribution and co-optation, as well as*

security apparatus maintenance. In other words, a gradual
bloating of the bureaucracy has played an important domestic
security function.[26]

King Hussein has also tried to secure the compliance of groups outside his regime's East Bank core. Unlike his Egyptian and Syrian counterparts, who have a history of antagonistic relations with the MB, King Hussein has sought to accommodate mainstream Islamists through political liberalisation, helping to underpin, rather than undermine, the status quo. Following nationwide food riots in April 1989, the MB's political wing, the Islamic Action Front (IAF), was granted political-party status. It took part in parliamentary elections later that year, winning most opposition seats and taking five government posts. This liberalisation has, however, been circumscribed and malleable: growing Islamist opposition to government policies prompted tighter political restrictions and a modified electoral law in 1993, making it more difficult for the IAF to win parliamentary seats.[27]

King Hussein has also tried to maintain the complicity of Jordan's Palestinians by safeguarding their basic security and livelihoods. As a result of immigration from the Israeli-occupied West Bank since the 1967 war, Palestinians accounted for an estimated 55–70% of the population in 1998. For King Hussein, the Palestinian issue is complex: while relying on East Bank Jordanians as his primary power-base, he must also integrate Palestinians with established roots in the East Bank; reconcile more recent Palestinian refugees to his regime; and position his regime in relation to Palestinians remaining in the West Bank.

Servicing the Military Constituency

Assad, Mubarak and King Hussein are attentive to the private and corporate concerns of their officer corps. While their service records may predispose them to sensitivity towards the military's corporate interests, providing benefits increases the support of the military establishment and weds officers to the status quo. In turn, this 'buys' the regime broader political autonomy; as one observer puts it, the Egyptian military 'is more than happy to stay out of politics as long as it can run its own economy'.[28]

Table 2 *Defence Expenditure in the Middle East and North Africa, 1985, 1996–1997*

	Expenditure			% of GDP		
(1997 US$m)	*1985*	*1996*	*1997*	*1985*	*1996*	*1997*
Algeria	1,357	1,840	2,114	1.7	4.0	4.6
Bahrain	215	295	364	3.5	5.4	6.5
Egypt	3,679	2,742	2,743	7.2	4.5	4.3
Iran	20,258	3,442	4,695	36.0	5.0	6.6
Iraq	18,328	1,277	1,250	25.9	8.3	7.4
Jordan	857	461	496	15.9	6.4	6.4
Kuwait	2,558	3,973	3,618	9.1	12.5	11.4
Lebanon	285	494	676	9.0	3.7	4.5
Libya	1,923	1,327	1,250	6.2	5.1	4.7
Morocco	913	1,431	1,386	5.4	3.8	4.2
Oman	3,072	1,957	1,815	20.8	12.5	10.9
Qatar	427	772	1,346	6.0	8.9	13.7
Saudi Arabia	25,585	17,730	18,151	19.6	12.7	12.4
Syria	4,961	2,132	2,217	16.4	6.4	6.3
Tunisia	594	406	334	5.0	2.0	1.8
UAE	2,910	2,115	2,424	7.6	5.2	5.5
Yemen	696	369	403	9.9	7.2	7.0

Note In 1997, the average expenditure for the region, including Israel and Mauritania, accounted for 6.9% of GDP. In comparison, NATO's expenditure was 2.2% of its member-states' total GDP; East Asia and Australasia's 4.7%; and Central and Southern Asia's 4.9%. The global average in 1997 was 2.7%.

Source *The Military Balance, 1998/99* (Oxford: Oxford University Press for the IISS, 1998), pp. 296, 300

Military perquisites take two broad forms: corporate benefits, including relatively high military budgets (see Table 2, page 25), weapon supplies and other material and symbolic rewards; and private benefits accruing to individual members of the high command or to the officer corps at large. Private benefits include disproportionately high wages paid to officers relative to other civil servants or the rank and file; housing and transport subsidies; access to scarce consumer goods; and the establishment of self-contained military cities such as those in Egypt, which provide access to subsidised consumer goods, high-quality medical care and transport facilities unavailable to the general population.

In general, the degree of attention paid to the military's welfare depends on the sensitivity of the unit in question and the gravity of any potential disaffection. After the 1980–88 Iran–Iraq War, Iraqi President Saddam Hussein took steps to nurture the army's support, including setting up

corporate and private military perquisites subsidised markets, giving highly decorated officers automobiles and lowering the criteria for admission into colleges and universities for members of the armed forces.[29] After the 1991 Gulf War, Saddam doubled salaries, eased the terms of military service and lowered the retirement age for officers.[30]

Smuggling networks between Lebanon and Syria, in which Syrian military and security personnel are allegedly involved, are a further example of private benefits. Since the mid-1990s, Assad has sought to crack down on drug-trafficking, which was a thriving business in the 1980s and early 1990s.[31] The Syrian military maintains a large presence in Lebanon's Bekaa Valley, where large amounts of opium and cannabis were cultivated and funnelled through networks purportedly controlled by some of Syria's top military and security officials. The value of opium-trafficking alone was estimated at $5 billion in 1991.[32] According to the US State Department, Syrian officials oversaw growing areas, approved shipments through military checkpoints and used military vehicles to transport processed drugs and raw opium plants to laboratories for conversion.[33] Syrian officers are also alleged to be involved in the thriving trade in consumer goods from Lebanon, as well as in outright plunder, confiscating houses, apartments, furniture and automobiles for personal use. Assad's periodic clampdowns on smuggling by his security chiefs may be designed to reduce the influence of the security and military apparatus.[34] At the same time, however, the regime may rely on these opportunities for private gain to keep the military content as weapons acquisition slows down. Between 1987 and 1997, the value of arms delivered to Syria fell from $2.7bn to $104m.[35] As a US military analyst put it in March 1998, 'The military may not get equipment, but they can fill their own pockets in Lebanon'.[36]

This smuggling raises important questions for Assad's foreign policy, specifically Syria's role in Lebanon. While withdrawal is unlikely for strategic reasons, it could also limit the incomes of Assad's allies and constituents in the military and security services. Assad's internal security needs may therefore reinforce the external security rationale for remaining in Lebanon. Trafficking in consumer goods may also undermine Assad's economic reforms. Foreigners wary of corruption and black-market activities may be less willing to invest in Syria. Assad mounted a particularly comprehensive crackdown in mid-1993 on the eve of two regional economic meetings; one analyst attributes the subsequent strengthening of the Syrian pound to the onset of the campaign.[37] However, Assad's attempts to secure the support of the military and security services may undermine his efforts to promote economic growth and increase the regime's social support in the long term.

Similarly, the Egyptian military's economic activities are vital to political control. Since the early 1980s, the Egyptian armed forces have become increasingly involved in military and non-military manufacturing, agricultural development, construction and land reclamation, as well as in service areas such as tourism.[38] In the past, these activities have been justified by the regime on the grounds that the military is best equipped to undertake them. However, individual officers can also benefit from extra income through ties with the private sector, and from opportunities for corruption: 'The huge amount of funds in circulation, with inadequate accounting supervision, virtually guarantees "leakage" into private pockets'.[39] In corporate terms, the military has attained virtual vertical integration, producing its own food, providing its own housing and medical care, and building its own holiday facilities.[40] Neither production undertaken by the military on its own behalf, nor that of its civil enterprises, is subject to the Central Accounting Authority.[41] In effect, the military operates an internal market independent of state regulation or oversight.

Egypt's arms industry, the largest in the Arab world, is an essential component of the military's economic activities. The sector had a stated capacity of $1.5bn annually in the 1980s; by the mid-1980s, around 30 principal factories and companies employing some 100,000 people were engaged in producing ordnance, ammunition and field-service equipment, as well as aircraft and vehicle assembly.[42] In theory, there are sound national-security reasons for developing an arms industry to meet domestic needs, as well as for export. In practice, however, the efficiency and profitability of Egypt's arms industries, particularly where more sophisticated programmes are concerned, are suspect.[43] Egypt's problems in absorbing and maintaining US-supplied equipment, and its inability independently to support its squadrons of sophisticated combat aircraft, make it doubtful whether the country can efficiently manufacture complex weapon systems. In most cases, outside suppliers could, at less cost, provide the same products as those indigenously manufactured; Egypt's locally produced US-designed *Abrams* M1A1 tank is one of the more glaring examples.[44] It is also doubtful whether indigenous arms production increases national income. For example, the substantial earnings from arms sales to Iraq in the 1980s went directly into military coffers insulated from national accounts.[45]

International arms deliveries can also help to preserve the military's loyalty. The Middle East remains the world's largest market in terms of value for direct sales of advanced weaponry. Deliveries were estimated to be worth $17bn in 1997, up from $15bn in 1996. This represents 34% of the global market.[46] Often, however, the arms procured appear designed to enhance military prestige, rather than to improve battlefield effectiveness. In 1997, Jordan began to take delivery of 16 F-16A/B combat aircraft from the US – at the expense of essential, albeit less glamorous, programmes to support, operate and maintain existing equipment and forces. Although the

military 'toys' help to maintain loyalty

aircraft are provided under the terms of a $220m leasing deal, to be paid for out of the US military aid allocation to Jordan, maintenance and support will absorb $60m annually – over 10% of Jordan's total military expenditure in 1997. Similarly, in discussions about the allocation of US military aid, Egyptian generals consistently lobby for high-technology, high-prestige weapon systems.[47] Egyptian officers allegedly receive substantial commissions from US companies, thereby possibly benefiting privately, as well as corporately, from the procurement process.[48]

Foreign military aid can help to underpin stability by making it easier for regimes to meet the corporate needs of their militaries. US Foreign Military Financing (FMF) for Egypt – the reward for Cairo's 1979 peace treaty with Israel – stood at $1.3bn in 1998; a further $800m was provided in economic assistance. This aid does not, however, come without risks for Mubarak's regime. Military assistance, combined with joint exercises such as the biannual *Bright Star* and US-sponsored training of Egyptian officers, can encourage links between the military and their US counterparts, thereby increasing the independence of the officer corps. Abu Ghazala's strongly pro-American views meant that he was regarded by Washington as a crucial supporter of its regional interests. As a result, Mubarak may have found it difficult to sideline the Defence Minister when, in the late 1980s, his international and domestic

Table 3 *Arms Deliveries to the Middle East, 1987, 1992–1997*

(1997 US$m)	1987	1992	1993	1994	1995	1996	1997
Egypt	2,430	1,234	1,531	1,283	1,982	1,669	1,100
Iran	2,295	953	1,203	417	522	417	800
Iraq	7,965	n.a.	n.a.	n.a.	n.a.	n.a.	n.a.
Kuwait	270	1,094	1,012	864	939	1,081	700
Libya	810	90	83	83	83	83	104
Saudi Arabia	9,728	10,815	8,728	7,769	9,032	9,439	11,001
Syria	2,700	427	295	147	177	94	104
UAE	189	382	503	428	913	678	626

Source *The Military Balance, 1998/99*, p. 272

Table 4 *Arms Orders and Acquisitions in Egypt, Jordan and Syria*

Supplier	Classification	Designation	Units	Order Date	Delivery Date
Egypt					
US	fighter, ground-attack	F-16C/D	46	1991	1994
US	fighter, ground-attack	F-16C/D	21	1996	1999
US	hospital ship	AH-64A	36	1990	1994
US	helicopter	UH-60L	2	1995	1998
US	helicopter	CH-47D	4	1997	1999
US	frigate	OH *Perry*	3	1997	1997
US	helicopter	SH-2G	10	1994	1997
US	frigate	*Knox*	4	1997	
US	main battle tank	M1A1	555	1988	1993
US	main battle tank	M1A1	80	1996	1999
Netherlands	armoured infantry fighting vehicle	YPR-765	611	1995	1996
Domestic	armoured personnel carrier	*Al-Akhbar*		1998	
US	artillery	SP 122	24		1998
US	surface-to-air missile	*Avenger*	50	1998	
US	armoured personnel carrier	M-113	378	1995	1997
Jordan					
US	fighter, ground-attack	F-16A/B	16	1995	1997
US	transport	C-130-H	1		1997
US	helicopter	UH-60L	4	1995	1998
US	tactical helicopter	UH-1H	18		1996
US	main battle tank	M-60A3	50		1996
US	main battle tank	M-60A3	38		1998
US	artillery	203mm	18		1998
Syria					
China	surface-to-surface missile	M-9			1997
Ukraine	main battle tank	T-55MV	200	1995	1997

Source   *The Military Balance*, 1998/99, pp. 119–21

popularity was growing. This may explain why Mubarak reportedly tries to limit US influence in the military by constraining the career paths of American-trained officers.[49]

US military aid to Jordan stood at over $50m in 1998. In addition to the 16 F-16s ordered from the US, the last of which was delivered in March 1998, Jordan took delivery of US military equipment valued at over $100m in 1996. This included 18 helicopters, 50 tanks, 250 light trucks, night-vision equipment and a C-130 transport plane. Jordan also received medical supplies, assault rifles and light trucks through the US Excess Defense Articles (EDA) programme, under which surplus US equipment is provided virtually free of charge to selected recipients.[50] In 1996, the US designated Jordan as a major non-NATO ally, giving it the same status as Australia, Egypt, Israel, Japan and South Korea, as well as priority consideration for EDA assistance.[51] The Jordanian military mounts joint exercises with US forces, and benefits from a substantial US-financed military-training programme.[52] Assistance such as this indirectly bolsters King Hussein's regime, while potentially reinforcing pro-Western sentiment among the military.[53] It also gives the military a vested interest in the Jordan–Israel peace treaty. This is significant given the population's general unhappiness over the accord's illusory 'peace dividend'. Washington's attempts to increase aid to Jordan therefore have important strategic ramifications for US regional interests: one of the 'specific objectives' of US aid is to ensure 'Jordan's continued participation in the Middle East peace process and regional co-operation with Israel'.[54] For similar reasons, cutting US military aid in the future could adversely affect Egypt's already chilly relations with Israel; as far back as the 1970s, credible US pledges to supply the Egyptian military with arms were crucial in gaining its complicity in Sadat's moves to secure peace.

Finally, regular attendance at military manoeuvres, graduation ceremonies and parades, as well as informal visits to bases and barracks, are essential if political leaders are to cultivate military support. Although leaders the world over show regard for their militaries, speeches and public appearances are particularly important in the Arab world. Public affirmations of the military's prerogatives and privileged status tend to become more frequent during periods of internal stress, when the military's services are likely to be called upon. After the demonstrations in Ma'an were suppressed in February 1998, King Hussein and other prominent officials publicly praised the integrity and honour of the country's armed forces. In the aftermath of the 1991 Gulf War, Saddam lavished praise on his military in public ceremonies and events and, contrary to his past reservations regarding creating military 'heroes', singled out individual commanders for their accomplishments.[55]

Stacking the Deck

Appointing individuals from the same religious, tribal, ethnic or regional group to key military positions is one of the most pervasive and effective ways by which political leaders secure the support of their armed forces. Appointees with a shared background help to ensure that the military's preferences are similar to those of the regime. Privileging these interests also creates a constituency with a vested interest in the status quo. In Syria, Jordan and Iraq, the groups underpinning the regime are all privileged minorities, which could be at risk under regimes governed by majority groups.

Assad relies principally on minority Alawis drawn from Latakia on Syria's north coast, although other minorities such as Christians and Circassians also tend to be over-represented in the military. An informal, Alawi-dominated core controls the main levers of power in the military and security services; over 90% of the key commands in the armed forces and security apparatus are held by Alawis.[56] Alawis prominent in the security forces include: Chief of Staff Ali Aslan; General Ali Duba, the Head of Military Intelligence; Mohammed al-Khawli, Head of the air force and former Chief of Air Force Intelligence; Adnan Makluf, former Commander of the Presidential Guard; and Ibrahim Safi and Shafiq Fayyad, commanders of the Second and Third Corps respectively.[57] Sunnis are well-represented in the rank and file and have a sizeable presence in the officer corps, but tend to be concentrated in administrative and technical-support positions and in the air force, rather than in the armoured and mechanised infantry units crucial for regime security.[58] Sunni officers also tend to be drawn from the rural lower classes, rather than from the urban middle classes. This rural–urban divide overlays sectarian divisions and is a central part of the regime's recruitment practices.

King Hussein relies on native East Bank tribes in the military at the expense of the Palestinian majority. Although the introduction of selective conscription in 1976 reportedly increased Palestinian representation among junior officers, East Bank Jordanians continue to provide the bulk of senior officers and to hold key command posts, especially those essential to regime security. As an additional safeguard, Palestinians entering the armed services are, like Syria's Sunnis, often channelled into technical services or into the air force; vital infantry and armour units are largely the preserve of East Bankers.

Like his Syrian and Jordanian counterparts, Saddam relies on a privileged minority: the Sunni who constitute 32–37% of the country's Arab population, compared with the 60–65% majority of the country's southern Shi'a.[59] His core support comes from Sunni Muslims from his home town of Tikrit, about 100 miles north of Baghdad, and from the network of closely allied tribes from Iraq's central 'Sunni heartland'.[60] Saddam has long reserved pivotal military posts for Sunnis, who have traditionally been over-represented in sensitive units and commands like the Republican Guard and Special Republican Guard, as well as in the officer corps in general. The regime draws on its Shi'i majority and on the Kurdish population to fill the lower ranks. However, since the 1991 Gulf War, Saddam has removed many Kurds and some Shi'i, indicating the contraction of his minority-based regime.[61]

Appointments are also heavily based on tribal and family links. Often the military's most sensitive command posts are filled by individuals with kinship or personal ties to the political leadership. Many of King Hussein's relatives occupy pivotal positions in the regime, including his cousin and fellow Hashemite General Zeid bin

kinship is key to élite control

Shaker, the long-serving Army Commander-in-Chief and former Prime Minister. King Hussein's son Prince Abdullah heads the Special Operations Command.[62] Many senior officers have traditionally been recruited from key rural tribes with which the King maintains personal relations. In Syria, membership of Assad's extended family and of select tribal subsections has been the key to securing sensitive senior appointments.[63] In Iraq, tribal affiliation reinforces the regime's sectarian foundations. Despite the fact that tribalism as a concept conflicts with *Ba'ath* Party ideology, Saddam has used tribal links since his time as leader of the Party's security apparatus under his predecessor Hasan al-Bakr's regime, when he filled key posts with members of tribes from Tikrit, and others such as the Jubbur and Ubayd.[64]

By the time he assumed the official title of President in 1979, Saddam had effectively colonised the security apparatus with these groups. During the Iran–Iraq War, he accelerated and expanded recruitment from other tribes and began publicly to resurrect the tribe as a primary organising principle for the regime.[65] Since the late 1980s, public affirmations of tribal fealty have increased as Saddam has granted symbolic and material concessions, including weapons, to tribal sheikhs.[66] Saddam has also sought to reinforce his links with Shi'i tribes and to strengthen those with traditional Sunni ones as a way of bridging the 'Sunni and Shi'i abyss' that played a prominent part in the 1991 Shi'i uprising against his regime.[67] Since the rebellion, Saddam has channelled resources to the Shi'i-dominated south.[68] At the same time, Saddam uses the *Ba'ath* Party, over which he retains organisational control, to balance tribal influence.

In theory, individuals with personal ties to the regime have the most to gain from supporting it, and the most to lose should it fall, particularly if they are implicated in its repressive activities. The Kurdish and Shi'i uprisings in the north and south of Iraq after the 1991 Gulf conflict failed partly because Sunni tribal groups temporarily put aside their differences with the regime to counter this dual threat. However, family or personal ties are no guarantee of loyalty. Since the mid-1990s, internecine squabbles within Saddam's extended family have prompted him to draw from a wider network, including from among the long-time *Ba'ath* Party faithful.[69] Rifaat al-Assad's bid for power against his brother in 1983–84 is a further indication that blood relations do not necessarily guarantee support.[70] Nonetheless, the tendency for family or tribal groups to unite against external opposition makes them a relatively reliable basis for organising the regime.

Managing the Military

Political leaders in the Arab world use a variety of more direct methods to maintain control over their militaries. These include removing undesirable elements through purges; developing special combat and intelligence units designated for internal security and headed by proven regime loyalists; and establishing institutional means to regulate the military establishment.

Purges

Purges are a powerful way of controlling the military's composition and safeguarding against opposition. They both remove unde- sirables, and demonstrate a regime's power and authority, thereby deterring would-be trouble-makers. After coming to power, almost all new leaders have eliminated or marginalised their former competitors' clients in the military. Nasser purged the army of supporters of General Nagib, the ousted first President of the Free Officers' regime; Sadat of Nasser's leftist allies; Assad of Jadid's followers; and Saddam of his rivals in the *Ba'ath* Party. Politically undesirable or potentially untrustworthy elements are also often removed. During his rise to power through the ranks of the *Ba'ath* Party, Assad participated in purges of sectarian and ethnic elements in the armed forces, especially Sunni after 1963, Druze three years later, Hawrani in 1966–68 and Ismaili in 1968–69.[71]

Purges are not confined to a regime's early years in power. 'Weeding' of the officer corps often takes place following the removal of a popular faction leader or rival. In the late 1960s, Nasser undertook a widespread purge designed in part to eliminate Field Marshal Amer's residual supporters.[72] In the absence of a clear challenge, purges also aim to pre-empt opposition to an unpopular policy initiative. In the run-up to Sadat's fateful trip to Jerusalem in 1977, 130 officers were retired or transferred.[73] Dozens of officers and men were reportedly sidelined as a result of their opposition to Assad's decision to fight against Palestinian forces in 1976. By 1980, Assad had transferred over 400 army officers in three separate waves in a bid to secure his military support-base during crackdowns on opposition forces.[74] In January 1982, during the Islamist suppression, reports emerged that 25 officers had been executed and 175 arrested for plotting a coup.[75]

The frequency, magnitude and brutality of purges vary considerably depending on the degree of anticipated or actual opposition and the extent to which other measures of control are in place. Since the 1950s, purges have been rare in Jordan; they were more common in Syria in 1976–82, and following Assad's confrontation with his brother in 1984, but have since become less frequent with the eclipse of the ideological divisions characteristic of the early independence period. By contrast, purges are regularly reported in contemporary Iraq.

Failing to root out competing factions or to identify potential coup-makers can itself prompt a challenge to the regime. The rise of the Free Officers' movement in Egypt and the spread of its cells in the military laid the groundwork for the July 1952 coup against Farouk. Nasser then purged many of Farouk's senior officers. In Jordan, King Hussein initially failed to appreciate the dangers posed by growing leftist sentiment in the late 1950s. Only when a coup was averted in 1957 did King Hussein move against its pro-republican perpetrators and their sympathisers. In Iraq, the inability of any single faction to sideline its competitors contributed to the country's cycle of post-independence coups, including the one that ousted the Hashemites in 1958. To secure his position, Saddam used his *Ba'ath* Party post to marginalise opponents in the 1960s and 1970s, gradually eliminating competing elements in the military.

Developing Internal-Security Agencies

Developing specific combat and intelligence units designated for internal security is another essential safeguard against military intervention in politics. These forces can be both stand-alone entities, such as Jordan's Royal Guard and Syria's Presidential Guard and Struggle Companies (*Saraya al-Sira*); and units formally part of the army command, but traditionally relied on for internal security.[76] Complementary intelligence organisations are attached to the services or to specific units, or act as stand-alone agencies. Egypt established agencies for military and general intelligence in the 1950s; since then, security and intelligence services have proliferated across the Arab world to permeate many aspects of military and civilian life. In general, internal security and intelligence organisations are well-equipped, commanded either by a leader's close personal associate or by an individual of demonstrated loyalty, and answer directly to the palace or the president.

Every state, whether democratic or authoritarian, has intelligence, counter-intelligence and internal-security agencies. However, in autocratic regimes these organisations tend to have overlapping mandates, and personal loyalty is emphasised. Other factors setting these agencies apart from their democratic counterparts include their selection criteria, lack of transparency and limited public accountability. Although each agency or entity usually has its own portfolio of responsibilities, combined they perform five crucial functions.

- *Monitoring*. Intelligence agencies and security services monitor the attitudes and activities of the military, other security services and civilian opposition groups. They may make arrests and interrogate those suspected of 'subversive' activities.
- *Defence*. Select combat units protect presidential and royal residences and offices. Loyal, trained and well-armed, they are also deployed if activity associated with a coup is detected, and to suppress opposition forces.
- *Prevention*. The proliferation of these agencies prevents each from growing too powerful and posing a threat to the regime. Internal rivalries and competition are commonplace, increasing the likelihood that threats from within the security and intelligence apparatus will be exposed. This also safeguards against the hoarding of intelligence by these organisations, ensuring that the best information reaches the top.
- *Balancing*. Security and intelligence services can constitute centres of power in their own right, coexisting or competing with the conventional armed forces. They therefore balance the military's influence, much as do non-military constituencies such as the party apparatus and bureaucracy.
- *Specialisation*. In assuming day-to-day responsibility for internal security, independent security services can sometimes free the military to focus on external enemies.

The resources, technology and methods available to the security and intelligence agencies make them highly effective at rooting out opposition and preventing coups. They increase the tactical challenges of launching a coup by making it difficult for an aspiring faction to build a network of sympathetic units without being discovered. Nasser and his Free Officers, for example, would find it tactically far more difficult to remove Mubarak than they did to topple Farouk.

Syria's elaborate security infrastructure consists of at least five conventional intelligence and security agencies; paramilitary or commando units dedicated to internal security; and 'political' military forces – combat units that play a supplementary internal-security role.[77] Rumours of competition and intrigue among and within the complex of security-related entities abound.[78] Military Intelligence, the country's largest and most powerful agency, also plays a major role in Lebanon through its Syrian Military Intelligence branch under Ghazi Kana'an. Assad is close to Air Force Intelligence, whose remit extends beyond its formal responsibilities to embrace civilian monitoring and

playing off parts of the military establishment

arrests, providing security at official functions and engaging in covert operations. Political Security and General Intelligence, with its feared Internal Branch, are also important. Although nominally civilian agencies, both are run by military officers and answer directly to Assad. The President's National Security Council acts as a coordinating office for these disparate entities. Among the regime's paramilitary or commando units, the 10,000-strong Presidential Guard plays a key role in garrisoning Damascus; one of its sub-units, Presidential Security, is commanded by Assad's son Bashar, who took over after the death of his elder brother Basil in 1994. Also important are units from the paramilitary Special Forces, the Struggle Companies and Unit 569, the remnant of Rifaat's Defence Companies.

Saddam's regime has numerous security agencies directly accountable to the President.[79] One of many powerful agencies, the Special Security Service, was formed in the mid-1980s; headed by Saddam's son Qusay, its main task is presidential security. General Intelligence and Military Intelligence, together with their sub-divisions and regional branches, are also key agencies, as are the General Security Service (secret police) and the Military Security Service.[80] An umbrella organisation, the Office of National Security, brings together representatives from the intelligence agencies in regular meetings. The 26,000-strong Special Republican Guard is the foremost paramilitary/military force involved in securing the regime. It protects the President's residence and provides mobile security; as a special emergency force, it is called upon to crush nascent rebellions. The Republican Guard's six divisions, once the most important internal force, play a supplementary role. Saddam's paramilitary Commandos, formed by his son Uday in 1995 and now led by Qusay, lack the equipment and training of the premier forces, but could be called on to support the regime in the event of social disturbances or to prevent a 'rolling coup' – uprisings that begin in one city and then spread to others.[81]

Unlike Syria and Iraq, security entities have not proliferated in Egypt. This may be due in part to historical factors: in the 1960s, Amer controlled Military and General Intelligence and may have been unwilling to sanction the growth of new agencies. The relative ethnic and religious homogeneity of Egyptian society may also have made it easier to protect against sectarian or ethnic factionalism in the military (99% of the population are of Eastern Hamidic stock; in terms of religion, 94% are Sunni Muslim, with the remainder primarily composed of Coptic Christians). Egypt has three main security and intelligence agencies: Egyptian General Intelligence; the Department of Military Intelligence; and the State Security Investigative Service. The regime also maintains a relatively small Presidential Guard, often reported as a single armoured brigade. Traditionally, its profile within the regime has been low. However, Defence Minister Field Marshal Mohammed Hussein Tantawi and Chief of Staff Magdy Hatata both come from the Presidential Guard, which may indicate that its influence is growing.[82]

The Egyptian regime also appears to maintain a firmer division between conventional military and internal-security functions. After the 1967 war, Nasser oversaw the expansion of the CPF, the regime's primary internal-security instrument. By his death, it numbered 100,000 personnel, rising to its present complement of some 300,000 under Sadat. The CPF, which is part of the Ministry of the Interior, leads the battle against Islamist militancy, thereby leaving the military largely free to focus on traditional combat responsibilities. Nonetheless, the military remains the ultimate guarantor of the regime, as demonstrated in 1977, when it helped to suppress protests over impending cuts in food subsidies, and again in 1986, when it was forced to quell CPF disturbances. In late 1997, it stepped in to assist the inept CPF command following an attack by Islamist militants at Luxor. A potentially worrying by-product of the military's 'professionalisation' is that it finds it distasteful to intervene in internal-security matters; it was not enthusiastic about suppressing the disturbances of 1977 and 1986, and in both instances quickly returned to barracks. Regimes like Mubarak's may seek to maintain a division of labour between their military and security forces, but they cannot afford to 'professionalise' to the point where their officers will no longer intervene in civil affairs on their behalf.[83] Given concerns about the CPF's competence and the possibility of future social unrest due to economic reforms – the repeal of urban and rural rent controls, the bedrock of the Nasserite social contract, and reductions in state employment – this reluctance to become involved in internal security matters could pose a problem for the regime.[84]

Jordan's well-equipped Royal Guard, established by King Hussein's uncle Sherif Nasser in the 1950s, plays a crucial role in protecting the regime, alongside the Special Forces Brigade, which emerged in the late 1960s; in 1996, these forces were merged under the newly formed Special Operations Command. Security forces are also housed within the Ministry of Interior's Public Security Directorate. Within General Headquarters in Amman, the Directorate of General Intelligence is the primary agency for collecting internal intelligence, along with its counterpart, Military Intelligence.

Institutional Checks
Arab regimes use a variety of institutional means to maintain control over the military establishment. In addition to a partisan approach to recruitment and dismissal – under which personal loyalty is a necessary and sometimes sufficient criterion for sensitive appointments – political leaders establish a centralised command and control structure, with complex checks and balances; make frequent command rotations; and maintain a large military.

Centralising authority prevents the development of independent power-bases and the emergence of charismatic leaders and factions. It also safeguards against subversive activities within the command by sharply limiting officers' scope for independent action. Under a centralised system, designated regime-security units such as Syria's Presidential Guard and Iraq's Special Republican Guard, service chiefs and army corps and division leaders report directly to the palace or the presidency, even if formal command structures call for them to be routed through the Minister of Defence or Chief of Staff. In wartime, operational command is often concentrated in the rear, with division or corps commanders maintaining substantial control over the activities of front-line forces.

As further insurance against independent action, complex checks are often built into command and control structures, sometimes resulting in the type of overlapping or parallel command systems established by communist parties. In the early 1970s, Saddam reputedly claimed that 'With party methods there is no chance for anyone who disagrees with us to jump on a couple of tanks and overthrow the government'.[85] During the early phases of the Iran–Iraq War, Saddam attached *Ba'ath* Party commissars to military units sent into battle in order to monitor their activities. Informal checks and balances often supplement or replace formal measures. In Syria, an Alawi officer may act as a 'shadow commander' in pivotal units led by non-Alawis; senior Alawi officers are tied to the high command and may communicate directly with the presidential palace.[86] Finally, checks and balances can be established through creative adjustments such as forming new layers in the command structure, compartmentalising decision-making in the services or in key military formations, requiring all significant decisions to be approved by a number of senior officers or by the head of state, and by marginalising suspect commands.

In most Western militaries, officers and commanders serve a term of duty, and are then rotated to new commands on a regular basis. In *posting rotations help to maintain central control* authoritarian regimes, command rotation is often governed by a political logic that is not always consistent with military needs. Rapid turnover in command prevents factions from emerging by moving officers before they can build a power-base. Saddam is reputed to have frequently rotated military personnel.[87] Mubarak also resorts to rotations to prevent senior officers from building

Table 5 *Force Sizes in the Middle East and North Africa, 1997*

('000)	Active	Reserve	Paramilitary	Total	% of Male Population (18–32 Years of Age)
Algeria	124	150	146.2	420.2	11
Bahrain	11	n.a.	9.9	20.9	33
Egypt	450	254	230	934	12
Iran	518	350	350	1,218	14
Iraq	387.5	650	55.4	1,092.9	37
Jordan	104	35	30	169	25
Kuwait	15.3	23.7	5.0	44	19
Lebanon	55.1	n.a.	18.5	73.6	13
Libya	65	40	0.5	105.5	14
Morocco	196.3	150	42	388.3	10
Oman	43.5	n.a.	4.4	47.9	20
Qatar	11.8	n.a.	n.a.	11.8	21
Saudi Arabia	162.5	n.a.	15.5	178	7
Syria	320	500	8.0	828	42
Tunisia	35	n.a.	12	47	4
UAE	64.5	n.a.	1.0	65.5	30
Yemen	66.3	40	80	186.3	9

Note   Population figures include nationals and non-nationals

Source   *The Military Balance, 1998/99*, p. 296

power-bases.[88] Assad, however, practises the opposite: entrenchment based upon demonstrated loyalty. Most of the prominent Alawis in command of the armed forces and of security and intelligence agencies in the early 1970s were in similar or closely related positions well into the 1990s, although some changes have been made, possibly to prepare the ground for Bashar's succession.[89] Occasionally, individuals appear to fall out of favour and seem to be stripped of their powers, only to have them restored later. This appears to have been the case with the long-time head of Military Intelligence, General Duba, who was reportedly removed in 1993, only to resume his post shortly afterwards. Similarly, Mohammed al-Khawli, who was removed in 1986 as head of Air Force Intelligence, later reemerged as head of the air force.[90] Although the character of the regimes may differ, both techniques – frequent turnover and entrenchment – have the same aim: to prevent the growth of factions within the military that might potentially challenge the regime.

Maintaining a large military establishment relative to population is a less obvious, but equally significant, way of maintaining political control over the armed forces (see Table 5, page 42). In Jordan, employment in the military offers additional benefits to the regime's native East Bank bedrock; the country's 104,000-strong active armed forces account for almost one-sixth of its adult male population between 18 and 32 years of age.[91] Military employment, like employment in the bureaucracy, thus plays a role in maintaining social support.

A large military also creates technical barriers to plotting a coup, which involves recruiting – in complete secrecy – a network of pivotal units with the access and mobility to detain the political leader and to seize control of all key communication systems and strategic points in the capital. It also requires a critical mass of officers and soldiers to support the takeover. A large and diversified army complicates efforts to establish this, and makes attempts to do so vulnerable to the intelligence and security services. Finally, a large military, accompanied by compartmentalised commands and a diversification of functions, also makes it more difficult for aspiring factions to build cross-cutting coalitions of supporters, and hence to develop a like-minded group with which to challenge the regime.

The political logic behind maintaining large militaries challenges the conventional view that significant military expenditure and sizeable armed forces are warranted in a region as volatile as the Middle East purely for national-security reasons. This view does not take into account the fact that many of the units in large militaries are under-equipped and inadequately trained. Syria maintains a force structure substantially larger than it can support, particularly with the end of Soviet aid.[92] In Egypt's case, Anthony Cordesman points out that the country 'attempts to support far too large an active force structure for its financial resources, and still maintains a large number of units with low grade Soviet-supplied equipment – which places a further burden on its inadequate logistic and maintenance system'.[93] Egypt's armed forces have numbered some 450,000 since the mid-1970s, despite the country's peace treaty with Israel.[94] Smaller and more efficient armies would make available scarce resources that could potentially be used to enhance military effectiveness. Similarly, the centralisation of command chains, purges, politicised appointment criteria and the tendency to select from privileged minorities all impose limitations on battlefield proficiency. As a result, leadership stability has in many cases been bought at the expense of military capability.

chapter 3

Political Control and Military Capabilities

The Arab world is home to many of the world's largest and most expensive militaries. These forces have rarely, however, realised their potential on the battlefield. In 1948, Arab armies fared poorly against Israeli forces; in the Suez imbroglio eight years later, Nasser's political victory obscured his military's mediocre performance; in the 1967 Arab–Israeli War, the coalition of Egyptian, Syrian and Jordanian forces failed to turn its substantial numbers of men and arms to its advantage. In the October 1973 war, Egypt squandered its initial strong position and the conflict ended with Egyptian forces in retreat. The Iraqi army only proved its mettle in the final phases of its war with Iran in the 1980s. Iraq's comprehensive defeat in 1991 again exposed the discrepancy between the country's order of battle and its actual capabilities.[1]

There are many reasons for this endemic military weakness, including budgetary problems, manpower limitations due to low literacy and education levels, difficulties in absorbing new technologies, poor training, inferior technology, erratic spare-parts supply and support systems, limited industrial development and the lack of a 'maintenance ethic'. Less appreciated is the impact of the methods regimes use to ensure political control over their militaries. This has crucial implications for a comprehensive assessment of the military balance in the Middle East.

Instruments of Political Control
Command Structures

Centralising power at the highest levels, depriving lower ranks of autonomy and otherwise tinkering with the chain of command for political reasons can have damaging effects on training and operations. The Egyptian command structure has been described as a 'tower with a pyramid on top'.[2] Each level has to query its superiors before approving any new initiative, which tends to create a stiff and unresponsive command. Command and control within the service branches is also extremely centralised. These and related problems are regularly reported by Western military officers acquainted with the Egyptian military.[3] There is little contact between the commands of the individual service branches, and ground and air force training and operations are poorly coordinated.[4] In the 1991 Gulf War, Egyptian forces rigidly adhered to orders, and found it difficult to be flexible in the field.[5] Egyptians themselves recognise these problems.[6] However, despite Western encouragement to devolve decision-making, the country's military command 'pays lip service to the American concept of delegating as much responsibility as possible to field commanders'.[7] After the 1997 *Bright Star* exercise with the US, the Egyptian military reportedly discussed the need to stimulate initiative and devolve command, but observers reported few signs that these proposals had been followed through.[8]

the problems of a rigid command

Rigidity of command is a particular difficulty at the strategic and theatre levels, although it can also undermine tactical proficiency if command and control problems lead to disintegration at lower echelons of the hierarchy. Command problems were a primary cause of the Egyptian military's poor performance in the 1967 war, when Egypt lost the Sinai Peninsula and Gaza Strip to Israel. Politically motivated convolutions in the chain of command introduced by Amer and Nasser caused confusion and wreaked havoc on deployments in the build-up to the conflict. Amer maintained control over operations, by-passing his high command and delivering instructions directly to division and brigade commanders in the field. Nasser was not given vital information and was apparently not involved in major decisions, including the disastrous order for the immediate withdrawal of Egyptian forces from the Sinai on 6 June: 'competing commands with overlapping responsibilities functioning in an atmosphere of little mutual cooperation had produced a disaster on the battlefield'.[9] The defeat was due to compromises Nasser had made to secure the loyalty of the military under Amer's command. As one observer put it, 'It has long been evident to military commentators that the principal Egyptian failure [in the 1967 war] was one of leadership. Given their equipment and numbers, the Egyptians should have done better than they did'.[10]

By the time the 1973 war with Israel broke out, Egypt's military capabilities had dramatically improved. Command problems nonetheless persisted. The conflict began with Egypt's textbook crossing of the Suez Canal, expelling Israeli forces from the Canal Zone and establishing a defensive line along the waterway. When Israeli forces breached this line in the second week of the war, Egypt's overcentralised and attenuated command structures prevented vital information from reaching the high command, and the significance of the breakthrough was missed. Subsequent Israeli offensives encircled the Egyptian Third Army on the Egyptian side of the Canal Zone.

Similar problems have undermined Iraqi capabilities. Analysts commonly cite overcentralisation and fragmentation of command as a major weakness, and attribute the country's early failures in the Iran–Iraq War to confused orders and a lack of fluidity in the command stemming partly from its politicisation. Iraqi battalion and brigade commanders, unwilling to take independent action, would defer to division or corps level, which in turn consulted the high command in Baghdad.[11] At the top, Saddam maintained control over operations, despite the fact that he had no real military experience and lacked the requisite skills. Saddam's tendency to emphasise static defence in operations made it easier for him to retain central control over his forces, rather than delegating substantial authority to front-line commanders. Significant authority was only delegated in the final phases of the conflict.

In Syria, 'lack of flexibility and speed of reaction in its high command' were evident both in the 1973 war with Israel and in the Lebanon conflict of 1982.[12] Michael Eisenstadt relates a particularly telling incident when, on the second day of the 1982 war, Assad sent his Deputy Chief of Staff for Operations, General Ali Aslan, from

Damascus to evaluate the military situation in Lebanon, rather than relying on local commanders. He thus 'wasted precious time and forfeited any possibility of responding in a timely manner to the rapidly unfolding events there'.[13] Syria's centralised command structure would almost certainly pose problems for coordination between and within the services in any large-scale operation.[14] The air force, Special Forces, Republican Guard, Struggle Companies and many of the army's other select units operate outside the formal chain of command, answering directly to Assad. This complicates coordination and encourages competition and open conflict.[15]

Selection Criteria

The premium placed on political loyalty in these regimes poses a dilemma in military appointments and promotions. A first – and fundamental – criterion in military appointments is sworn loyalty to the presidency or monarchy; a second is military talent and skill. Although individuals can meet both criteria, this order of priorities often leads to the appointment and promotion of men of impeccable political credentials, but less notable military expertise. The Egyptian command is a good example of the effects of political selection criteria on military leadership. Since the removal in 1989 of Field Marshal Abu Ghazala, the powerful and charismatic Defence Minister, Mubarak has maintained a colourless command in which key posts are filled by individuals described as 'weak people'; Western officers describe lacklustre meetings with service chiefs.[16] Although the officer corps benefits from American military training, officers may be denied speedy promotion to prevent the growth of US influence. 'If anything', notes an observer, 'US-trained officers have been subjected to a form of loyalty testing, whereby they are expected to remain silent when commanded by less competent, less well trained senior officers.'[17] This prevents the wider military from benefiting from the skills Egyptian officers acquire in foreign military academies: 'the failure to promote US-trained officers into high command positions has entailed a cost to military capability and professionalism'.[18]

selection by loyalty, rather than talent

In Iraq, Saddam's stringent application of political over military appointment criteria meant that his attack on Iran in 1980 was undertaken by a command with no real military experience or training.[19] Consequently, Iranian forces were able to mount a counter-offensive which retook Khoramshahr, the last major Iraqi stronghold on Iranian territory, in May 1982. Severe penalties meted out to the officer corps for incompetence, outspokenness or, paradoxically, for success (which could confer hero status and political popularity) further subdued independent thinking and action.[20] In the high command, this reportedly produced 'a situation in which Saddam Hussein's strategic decisions and way of handling the war were not seriously criticized by the military leadership who dared not challenge his authority'.[21] The extensive monitoring of the military and the punishments handed out to dissenting officers or enlisted men also encourage passivity in command. Military leadership must be practised with an eye to political survival, fostering a 'yes-man' mentality and deceit and concealment in the chain of command.[22]

Before 1970, in-fighting in Syria's *Ba'ath* Party meant that military experience and attention to duty were almost universally ignored in promotions. Although Assad reintroduced professional criteria in promotions in the early 1970s, politics remained an issue, even in the country's 'élite' forces, including those units of the well-armed and trained Defence Companies that were active in the 1973 war and later in Lebanon.[23]

Sectarianism and Tribalism

Using religious and tribal affiliation as selection criteria can deprive a regime of crucial manpower resources. In Jordan, the number of Palestinian conscripts in the armed forces has traditionally been carefully regulated. Palestinians also tend to be excluded from sensitive posts, despite the fact that they are generally better educated and more highly skilled than the Transjordanians on whom King Hussein relies. By limiting Palestinian representation in the most rigorously trained and well-equipped units, the regime deprives itself of some of its most capable manpower. In Syria, although large numbers of Sunni Muslims are present in the military, rural minority groups are preferred in the most sensitive posts.

During the Iran–Iraq War, Saddam recruited the majority of his senior officers from Sunni Muslim tribes, while the bulk of the rank and file were Shi'i. Attempts to increase manpower, together with concerns about loyalty, prompted Saddam to draw heavily on *Ba'athist* militiamen as front-line fighters, despite their poor quality. Since the 1991 Gulf War, Saddam's use of sectarian and ethnic principles has increased. Disaffection within the military has prompted the regime 'to "exempt" its Kurds and some of its Shi'ites from military service, for internal security forces – depriving it of a substantial part of its manpower base'.[24] Although the Iraqi army has never been manned according to its organisational tables, these exemptions further limit the selection pool. This, combined with other measures such as lowering the retirement age to bolster military loyalty and other manpower-related problems, has led some analysts to estimate that between a third and a half of the Iraqi army's order of battle consists of hollow forces.[25]

Military Perquisites

The military's involvement in commercial activities also has implications for its professionalism. After the 1967 war, the Egyptian military itself acknowledged the detrimental effect of its involvement in the state's political and military affairs, and its redefinition of its corporate interests was instrumental in the military 'professionalisation' which took place in the 1970s. Since the early 1980s, however, the military's political influence has rebounded and its economic activities have increased.[26]

Involvement in commercial enterprises can undermine training, readiness and discipline, especially when it involves corruption and opportunities for private gain. In Egypt, these effects are mitigated by efforts to maintain a division within the military between the economic activities of the Defence Ministry and those of the traditional combat services. Nonetheless, the military's involvement in commerce has been controversial, both with the civilian opposition and with elements of the armed forces.[27] Military participation in commercial activities may act as a form of political control precisely because it undermines the military establishment's cohesion; by creating a class of military entrepreneurs 'whose professional links are more likely to be with other entrepreneurs than with the army they serve', allegiances are divided and the

military entrepreneurs corrode military efficiency

status quo is reinforced.[28] In this way, the military's involvement in commercial activities illustrates the dilemma between sustaining political control and maintaining military effectiveness.

The alleged involvement of Syrian forces in black-market activities and corruption in Lebanon raises concern about military discipline and operational readiness among the 35,000–40,000 troops stationed there.[29] Actual manning levels are significantly lower than organisational charts suggest, possibly because personnel are engaged in commercial, rather than military, activities.[30] Economic rivalry between factions makes it difficult to develop a 'corporate identity' in the armed forces.[31] The impact of commercialism has had important strategic implications; according to a high-ranking US diplomat and former Reagan administration official, 'Syria's involvement in Lebanon has been a major help to peace [that is, absence of war with Israel] because of its effects on the Syrian military'.[32]

Finally, in all these regimes the lack of legislative oversight encourages bureaucratic parochialism and means that there is little transparency in decisions affecting military procurement. Accurate budget figures are seldom published; when they are, major categories of expenditure are excluded or subject to arcane accounting procedures. There are few external checks on investment in high-technology systems and few tools to control spending by the services, to rationalise policy or to reconcile procurement priorities with development goals. The military fiercely defends this freedom from legislative oversight; often the president or king will also do so on its behalf. When issues of military accountability are raised, they are interpreted as a sign of civil–military friction.[33] In the mid-1980s, Mubarak's sanctioning of parliamentary debate about military prerogatives was interpreted as a sign of friction between the President and the powerful Abu Ghazala.

Sources of Reform

The dilemma posed by the conflicting demands of political control and battlefield efficiency is more pronounced at certain times than at others. Two related factors strengthen a regime's hand against the military and enable it to undertake reform: an upsurge in popular support for the regime, or the incorporation of new interest groups; and the elimination of politically powerful factions in the military.

The dramatic improvement in Egyptian capabilities in the 1973 war stemmed from these factors. The roots of the reform process go back to 1967 and the mass outpouring of support Nasser received after his resignation speech on 9 June 1967. This, combined with popular disillusionment with the military after its dismal performance in the war, allowed Nasser definitively to sideline the powerful Amer and his clique. The President subsequently reclaimed the right to make appointments and promotions, undertook large-scale purges of officers and reformed the high command. Sadat continued the reform process by pressing on with economic liberalisation, thereby expanding the regimes' social bases, and by preventing new 'power centres' from emerging in the armed forces. Through these means, Sadat was able to retain the upper hand over his military.

Maintaining social support and eliminating contenders for power can lessen the need for measures detrimental to battlefield efficiency, but does not free these regimes from the need to cultivate military support. Hence, even as the military's 'professionalisation' proceeded under Sadat, the President used corporate benefits to gain its acquiescence in his peace initiatives with Israel. Sadat sought to rejuvenate Egypt's arms industry, which had stagnated under Nasser, under the auspices of the regionally funded Arab Organisation for Industrialisation (AOI); this initiative failed when the Gulf States turned against Egypt after the 1979 peace treaty with Israel. At the same time, the military budget dramatically increased. Sadat also used his powers of appointment to ensure the loyalty of his command.[34]

In Iraq, Saddam began tinkering with the architecture of political control after the Iranian counter-offensive in 1982 by purging 'incompetents', removing Party officials from the command structure and recalling officers removed for political reasons. Following Iran's capture of the Iraqi port and former oil terminal of Al Faw in early 1986, Saddam delegated control over military operations to his high command and allowed the generals to expand the Republican Guard with forces from regular army units of proven skill and competence.[35] Even while supporting reform, Saddam established safeguards against potential opposition from within the military by expanding the role and number of internal security forces.[36] Military reform appears to have continued after the end of the war with Iran in 1988. Since the 1991 Gulf War, however, Saddam has again tightened his personal control over the armed forces in response to growing military disaffection, and his 'reluctance to grant officers much independence of action' remains one of many important barriers to the realisation of Iraq's combat potential.[37]

The calibre of the Arab world's armed forces varies according to country, regime, service branch and battlefield context.[38] Nonetheless, across the region centralising command, creating overlapping commands, politicising selection criteria and authorising involvement in economic activities all compromise military effectiveness. In a volatile region like the Middle East, maintaining political control involves a substantial trade-off in military effectiveness, one that the region's leaders appear consistently willing to make.

chapter 4

Challenges to Stability:
Leadership Succession

Leadership succession is one of the most profound threats to regime stability in the Arab world. Since the 1991 Gulf War, the issue has come to the fore in discussions of Iraq, with fears of disintegration and civil war overshadowing speculation about Saddam's removal. PA leader Yasser Arafat's trembling hands, frequent bouts of fatigue and incoherence raise questions about his health, prompting analysts to single out possible successors. Assad grooms his son Bashar for power in a country where the coup is an established mechanism for leadership change. Although a Hashemite will probably inherit King Hussein's throne in Jordan, he will nonetheless have to consolidate power in his own right. Even in Egypt, which has managed two relatively smooth leadership transitions, Mubarak's failure to select a Vice-President leaves him without a designated successor.

The uncertainty surrounding succession can prompt social turbulence as opposition groups seek to advance their claims, military factions compete with one another and the masses, responding to the leadership vacuum, seek to protect their basic livelihoods. At best, a relatively smooth transfer of power takes place, either to a designated successor, or to a figure enjoying enough confidence among the military and political élite to make his regime viable. At worst, the process collapses and serious conflict ensues. In Qatar in 1995, Emir Hamad bin Khalifa pushed aside his father in a bloodless palace coup; in Algeria, the annulment of elections in 1991, won by the Islamist *Front Islamique de Salut* (FIS), precipitated armed rebellion.

The military will play a crucial role in the Arab world's impending successions, whether explicitly or from behind the scenes. To manage these changes effectively, incoming leaders will need to cultivate and maintain social support to balance military influence; they also must ensure the backing, or at least acquiescence, of the armed forces. The methods used by the current generation of Arab leaders to control their militaries are likely to be just as important to their successors.

Syria

The succession question in Syria is among the most urgent. The elderly Assad (he was born in 1930) is widely reported to suffer from serious heart problems, diabetes and other ailments. Unlike Egypt, Syria has never enjoyed a leadership transition without a coup, nor does it share Jordan's monarchical tradition.

Assad's efforts to groom his eldest son Basil as his successor came to an end in 1994 with the younger man's death in a car accident. Basil's image had appeared frequently alongside his father's on posters in Damascus, and he had been given command of the key Presidential Security unit

power must be earned, not just inherited

charged with protecting the Assad family and high officials. Following Basil's death, Assad shifted his attention to his younger son Bashar. By 1995, Bashar's image was appearing alongside those of his father and late elder brother. Bashar, who was completing his residency as an ophthalmologist in London at the time of his brother's death, was given a swift course at Syria's military academy and assumed command of his brother's former unit. Bashar has also followed his brother in playing a high-profile role in Lebanese affairs, and has been associated with anti-corruption campaigns in an effort to establish a reputation for probity.[1]

However, most analysts agree that Bashar lacks his brother's charisma, stature and military experience.[2] Moreover, he will only reach 40, the minimum age for assuming the presidency, in 2006 (see Appendix, page 77). Amending this constitutional provision is possible, but would undermine Bashar's standing; in any case, the conventions of Syrian politics require power to be earned, not simply inherited. According to a veteran Syria-watcher, 'this is no monarchy … no one is going to passively accede to an Assad dynasty'.[3] As a result, it is unclear whether Bashar could quickly and decisively consolidate power upon Assad's departure.

Those sceptical of Bashar's prospects commonly forecast a collective leadership of Alawi military and security chiefs, perhaps with a Sunni façade or with Bashar as a figurehead. Individuals put forward for membership of this putative clique include Ibrahim Safi and Shafiq Fayyad, the commanders of the Second and Third Corps respectively; Ali Aslan, the Chief of Staff; Ali Duba, the head of Military Intelligence; Ibrahim Huwaji, the head of Air Force Intelligence; and his uncle, Mohammed al-Khawli, the air force chief.[4] Prominent Sunnis, such as Vice-President Khaddam and former Chief of Staff Shehabi, are commonly cited as possible compromise candidates, or as front men for the Alawi core.[5]

The power-struggle between Assad and his brother Rifaat in 1983–84 may indicate how such a succession could unfold. Angered at Assad's failure to include him on the six-strong team appointed to administer state affairs during his illness, Rifaat organised opposition among the country's Alawi generals, who were anxious to protect their positions against any challenge from the Sunni majority. Only after Assad recovered did the generals abandon Rifaat. Units of the Special Forces and Republican Guard confronted Rifaat's forces on the streets of Damascus, forcing him to abandon his bid for power. This suggests that, in Assad's absence, the regime's sectarian underpinnings may again prompt the Alawi élite to close ranks to ensure a smooth succession.

It is unclear, however, whether this coterie would last, or degenerate into intra-Alawi competition. The alliances and counter-alliances that Assad has encouraged in the armed forces to ensure political control could cause divisions between the Alawi generals in a succession. This could allow sections of the Sunni community, economic interests or other groups into the struggle for power as competing generals seek to build support outside of the Alawi core. The prospects for a collective leadership would in part depend on the level of opposition it faced from the Sunni majority: the greater the challenge, the more compelling the need to band together against it. There are few signs to suggest Sunni opposition on the scale of the MB's violent challenge in the 1970s and 1980s, while the regime has not signed up to an unpopular peace treaty with Israel. Assad's economic reforms have spurred growth and helped to bolster the Sunni commercial classes, potentially giving them a vested interest in the status quo. However, despite Assad's efforts to maintain support, the Sunni majority remains largely disenfranchised. Sunnis could thus provide a potential pool of opposition to the regime in a succession crisis. The exclusion of Sunnis from sensitive posts deprives them of a base within the military with which to organise a bid for power. Instead, the movement would have to assume the form of a mass insurrection; even well organised and supplied rebellions of this nature are difficult to achieve.

The nature of the post-Assad regime, and the degree to which Bashar succeeds in consolidating power, will in part depend on how and when Assad leaves office. If Assad lives for several years after his retirement, Bashar may have time to build his own military and civilian power-bases. Assad's selective use of appointments and other institutional prerogatives may in the meantime increase Bashar's chances. Assad has apparently begun to shape a military command receptive to his son's leadership, including weeding potential critics out of the regime. The most widely cited example of this process is the removal of Ali Haydar, the long-serving Special Forces commander, in July 1994 following his apparent criticism of Bashar, the peace process with Israel and his lack of promotion.[6] In August 1994, 16 officers, many of whom had been in their positions since the 1970s, were sidelined. Subsequently, a number of pivotal reassignments and personnel changes were made.[7] This 'wide-ranging and systematic reshuffle' was widely interpreted as partly a 'response to the thorny question of succession'.[8] One observer noted that:

> In light of … Asad's apparent desire to promote Bashar's
> Candidacy, Asad [appeared] anxious to remove personalities
> who were too well entrenched and too independent and could
> threaten Bashar's chances of establishing himself as a
> candidate for succession.[9]

Further changes were made in mid-1998. Bashir al-Najar, the Chief of General Intelligence, was removed, while Shehabi was retired having reached the mandated age of 67.[10] Shehabi's retirement may indicate that Assad is using the inevitable generational change in Syrian politics to pave the way for Bashar.

One of the most notable casualties of this process has been Rifaat, who was stripped of the Vice-Presidency in February 1998. Some analysts interpreted Rifaat's ousting as designed permanently to quash his aspirations to succeed his elder brother. Through his extensive commercial enterprises abroad and his media holdings, Rifaat had made an intellectual claim to power and was reportedly in the process of re-establishing contacts with the military and the business community in anticipation of Assad's departure from office.[11] Other analysts argued that Rifaat was more of an irritant than a threat, and that his removal was no more than good housekeeping.[12]

A third more interesting interpretation, put forward by the business press, linked Rifaat's removal to a resurgent interest in economic reform. Rifaat was widely alleged to have used questionable business practices, and his dismissal may have been designed to clear the decks before the possible advent of a government in which technocrats would play a more substantial role. Anticipated changes included greater efforts to settle Syria's debt arrears and to reform the financial sector.[13]

economic rationales for personnel changes

The fact that the Damascene business community saw Rifaat's removal, as well as other regime changes, as a signal to the commercial sector is significant given the broader social changes prompted by Syria's slow but steady economic liberalisation. By encouraging the commercial élite, Assad may be trying to create space in the regime for Bashar. Assad has apparently identified the networks between the public sector and the military and security forces as a principal barrier to Bashar's succession, and may be seeking to create additional sources of support from which his son could draw.[14] In this way, Assad's economic liberalisation may be addressing both the economic and the political future of his country. Even if these reforms fail to enhance Bashar's standing with the middle classes, if he assumes the leadership during a period of growth and stability, rather than of uncertainty and decline, he may have a better chance of consolidating power.

Ultimately, the shape of the immediate post-Assad leadership will depend upon how the regime's military and civilian elements combine. With his own group of supporters, Bashar would be in a position to act as a compromise candidate between the factions within the military and security services. Even so, he will have to rely on the Alawi generals until he expands his own following in the military, eliminates potential challengers and establishes a broader base for his rule within the *Ba'ath* Party and other constituencies.

In the event of a succession crisis in the near future, power seems likely to be assumed by a collective leadership of the Alawi security and military élite, with a Sunni façade or with Bashar as a figurehead. In the long term, the consolidation of power by a new leader, whether Alawi or not, depends on his capacity to cultivate social support, to satisfy the corporate interests of the military establishment and its officers' private interests, to appoint allies to sensitive posts, to purge 'suspect' elements and to otherwise guard against the emergence of competitors in the military. In the interim, until a new leader emerges and consolidates power, Syria may be vulnerable to competition among its Alawi chiefs, *Ba'ath* Party officials, the Sunni religious majority and mass economic and social constituencies. Given Syrian society's heterogeneity, these factors could profoundly threaten the country's internal stability.

Egypt

Since taking office in 1981, Mubarak has proved himself a resilient leader. He has successfully battled Islamist militants, and initiated a controversial economic-reform programme. By late 1998, he appeared to face no major competitors for power. In addition, Egypt has managed two relatively smooth leadership successions.

Mubarak is not, however, invulnerable. He narrowly escaped assassination by militant Islamists in Addis Ababa, Ethiopia, in 1995, and periodic attacks against high-ranking officials by Islamist militants, such as the 1994 assassination of Major-General Ra'uf Khayrat, a key officer in the State Security Investigative Service, raise the possibility of his untimely death. His appointment of a Vice-

President would not eliminate the uncertainty surrounding his succession. There are constitutional guidelines (see Appendix, page 77), but these tend to be quite malleable in authoritarian regimes; they are subject to formal abrogation or informal reinterpretation, and provide no firm indication of the way in which events might unfold.

While generally smooth, Egypt's past leadership changes have not been trouble-free. Nasser took power in 1954 only after winning a lengthy contest with General Nagib, and weathered a simmering two-month power-struggle with Amer in 1967 before the Field Marshal's arrest for coup-plotting. The removal of Amer and his faction paved the way for the relatively smooth transition to Sadat's rule in 1970. Even so, Sadat had to fend off a leftist-sponsored challenge in 1971, and his succession was not a foregone conclusion.

The military will play a key role in choosing Mubarak's successor. Precedent suggests that his heir will be either a military officer, or will have military credentials. Even if a civilian emerged as front-runner, the military would retain the right of veto. At the height of his powers in the mid-1980s, Abu Ghazala may have been well-positioned to assume the presidency.

Abu Ghazala's rise to power illustrates how a military contender could emerge. He was appointed Defence Minister by Sadat in 1981 and, during his lengthy tenure, protected the armed forces, particularly their economic activities, from political oversight, lobbying successfully to keep the military budget high and allegedly turning a blind eye to corruption in military enterprises. In late 1985, Mubarak began a campaign aimed at removing him, but was forced to abandon it under pressure from the US, which approved of Abu Ghazala's ardently pro-Western stance. The military's role in suppressing the CPF riots of 1986 strengthened Abu Ghazala's hand against Mubarak.[15] Only in 1989, under the guise of military reforms consistent with Egypt's IMF-sponsored economic programme, was Mubarak finally able to dismiss him.[16] Abu Ghazala was so imposing a figure that Mubarak was forced publicly to affirm that he was not removed to pre-empt a

uncertainty over Mubarak's successor seems almost deliberate

coup attempt.[17] Even after his dismissal, Abu Ghazala remained a powerful figure and retained links with former officers, but any political aspirations he may have harboured were quashed by the discovery of compromising videotapes of his sexual activities. Mubarak appears to have 'learned his lesson from Ghazala' and has since appointed individuals who are 'politically safe'; the lack of an obvious contender appears deliberate.[18] Abu Ghazala's successor as Defence Minister, General Yusif Sabri Abu Taleb, was commonly described as a quiet technocrat; his successor, Field Marshal Tantawi, reportedly also lacks Abu Ghazala's appeal. Although there are sound political reasons for these appointments, the absence of a realistic contender capable of commanding a substantial following in the armed forces increases the uncertainty surrounding Mubarak's succession.

Egypt's economic reforms raise concerns about possible social unrest during a change in leadership. Since the early 1990s, austerity measures under Egypt's economic-reform programme have brought macroeconomic stability, and the regime has embarked on a moderate but controversial structural-reform programme in which 314 public-sector companies have been slated for privatisation. Official unemployment rates were 8.8% in mid-1998, down from the double-digit figures of the 1980s; inflation stood at 4–5%; and 5% economic growth was forecast for 1998.[19] However, critics voice concerns about the distributional effects of the reforms; while a newly enriched class of entrepreneurs and business people has clearly benefited from the reforms, it is not clear that wealth is 'trickling down' to the impoverished classes. At the same time, the lower classes are forced to endure measures like the repeal of rural and urban rent controls – a centrepiece of the regime's social contract since the 1950s. Sceptics are concerned that disillusion is fostering discontent, and could potentially lead to upheavals on the scale of the 1977 bread riots or the 1986 CPF rebellion.[20]

The prospect of popular opposition to the reform process has implications for political–military relations. Opposition invites repression, shifting the balance of power in the military's favour. In the context of an uncertain succession, this is all the more important: a vacuum at the top increases the likelihood that people will take to the streets, or that opposition groups will become more assertive if the military is internally divided. A leadership vacuum could also bring any latent factionalism within the armed forces to the surface.[21]

Evidence that discontent over widening economic disparities may have spread to the military is of even greater concern. Observers report resentment among officers at their stagnating salaries, while the entrepreneurs and 'middle men' benefiting from economic deregulation become ostentatiously wealthy. An Egyptian major-general, a common senior-officer rank, earns about $300 a month, significantly less than a successful business person in the private sector. These issues are sensitive and are not discussed openly, although in June 1998 a knowledgeable Western official described reports of shouting in internal meetings over salaries and officer benefits, suggesting that disaffection is deepening.[22] Mubarak seems to have calculated that he can afford to withhold benefits, rather than allowing salaries and perquisites to grow substantially as he did in the 1980s. This may testify to his confidence in the other methods used to secure political control, and his belief that the newly emboldened commercial classes will bolster the regime against a restive officer class. At the same time, while not increasing salaries, the regime has not gone so far as to challenge other basic military perquisites. Benefits like the military hospital opened at al-Arish in June 1998 continue.[23]

The possibility that the military will assume a greater role in ensuring internal security is also a cause for concern. Traditionally, policing Islamist militants has been left to the CPF, with the armed forces providing logistical and other support.[24] However, security plans developed in the wake of the attack at Luxor by the militant Islamic Group in November 1997, in which 58 foreign tourists and four Egyptians were killed, apparently called for the military to play a more active, albeit supplementary, role in policing regions where militant activity is at high levels.[25] Factionalism within the Islamic Group could increase the need for greater overt military support to the CPF as break-away groups plot independent attacks.[26] The regime has nonetheless been careful to downplay the extent of the military's involvement in internal-security affairs.[27] Mubarak has good reason to be wary of actively involving the military in battling opposition forces, since doing so risks fuelling internal debate over domestic security strategy, creating tensions within the armed forces. Moreover, an increased military role in internal security could heighten its visibility and influence in the regime.[28]

Finally, the question of Islamist infiltration of the armed forces may become increasingly important in an uncertain succession, where the loyalty of junior officers and of the rank and file is crucial to efforts by competing leaders to build a support-base. There is no conclusive evidence as to the extent to which Islamists have infiltrated the military. While alarmist assessments need to be treated with scepticism, Islamist militant organisations clearly recognise that infiltrating the military is a key to success.[29] In 1993, leaders of the Vanguards of the New Jihad suggested that this was a major component of their strategy.[30] Islamist forces may have infiltrated the highest ranks of the security forces.[31] Arrests and round-ups of suspected activists have occasionally included enlisted men and junior officers; conscription means that many of the rank and file come from social classes in which militant sentiment is most likely to be present.[32] In response to concerns that Islamists may have infiltrated the CPF, the regime deploys Cairo-based conscripts in al-Minya, Asyut and other provinces in which levels of militant activity are high.[33] The regime can also use institutional safeguards (a centralised command, political appointment criteria and monitoring) to insulate itself from pro-militant tendencies among the lower ranks of the military.

Although the prospect of social tumult and Islamist militancy is a serious concern, other factors offer cause for optimism in evaluating Egypt's chances for a smooth succession. The armed forces retain a vested interest in maintaining their military and non-military economic activities, and receive significant amounts of sophisticated arms through FMF. The military's corporate welfare is therefore well provided for. The tenure of Mubarak's successor will depend on his ability to maintain this flow of resources to the military, while alleviating the apparent disaffection in its ranks, as well as in society at large. Much like Mubarak, he will secure himself by building social support, sidelining challengers in the armed forces and ensuring that the military's private and corporate interests are preserved.

Jordan

King Hussein's hospitalisation in mid-July 1998 for cancer treatment, his second bout of the disease since 1992, renewed concerns about Jordan's leadership succession. These concerns notwithstanding, on the surface at least Jordan's chances for a smooth succession appear good.

King Hussein's illness deepens succession worries

King Hussein has a designated heir, his younger brother Crown Prince Hassan, who has held this position since 1965. Most observers agree that the native East Bank Jordanians and the military appear prepared to support Hassan and continued Hashemite rule.

A smooth succession with Hassan at the helm is not, however, assured. Competition within the Hashemite family could be destabilising. As a Jordanian journalist put it in June 1998, the Royal Family is engaged in a 'subtle but vicious game over who will ascend the throne'.[34] Queen Noor reportedly supports her son, Hamza, as Hussein's successor. Moreover, although King Hussein has repeatedly reaffirmed Hassan as his designated successor, and in August 1998 delegated to him unprecedented authority over domestic affairs, Jordanians, and outside observers, speculate that he will instead pass the throne to one of his sons or another family member.[35] In a public letter to Hamza sent on his eighteenth birthday in 1998, King Hussein described the challenges he faced in assuming the throne when he was eighteen.[36] The letter was interpreted by some Jordanians as raising the possibility of offering the throne to Hamza. Other possible candidates include Prince Ali, the King's son by his third wife, Queen Alia. Hassan's son Rashid or one of the sons of King Hussein's brother Mohammad are also commonly cited as key players in the Jordanian succession.

Even if Hassan assumes the throne, the succession question will be merely delayed, not resolved. King Hussein has left the question of the future line of succession unanswered. In a televised interview with the BBC in 1993, King Hussein stated that 'The choice [of Hassan as his successor] was made a long time ago and I think it was the right choice. As for the future it will have to take care of itself'.[37] In October 1994, King Hussein called for the establishment of a council of the Hashemite family to decide on Hassan's successor.[38]

Figure I *King Hussein's Branch of the Hashemite Line*

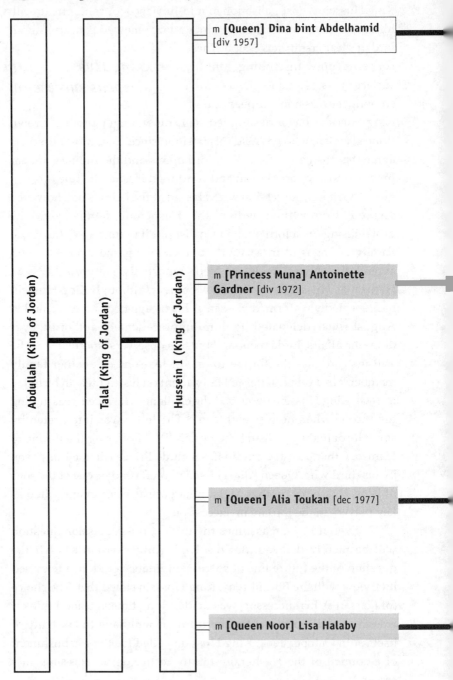

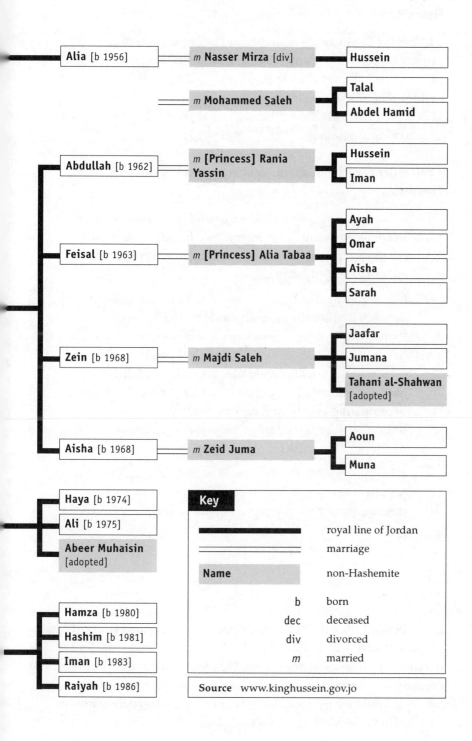

Key

royal line of Jordan

marriage

Name — non-Hashemite

b — born
dec — deceased
div — divorced
m — married

Source www.kinghussein.gov.jo

Figure 2 *Article 7 of the Jordan–Israel Peace Treaty, 26 October 1994*

1 Viewing economic development and prosperity as pillars of peace, security and harmonious relations between states … the Parties, taking note of understandings reached between them, affirm their mutual desire to promote economic cooperation between them, as well as within the framework of wider regional economic cooperation.

2 In order to accomplish this goal, the Parties agree to the following:

a To remove all discriminatory barriers to normal economic relations, to terminate economic boycotts directed at each other, and to cooperate in terminating boycotts against either Party by third parties.

b Recognising that the principle of free and unimpeded flow of goods and services should guide their relations, the Parties will enter into negotiations with a view to concluding agreements on economic cooperation, including trade and the establishment of a free-trade area, investment, banking, industrial cooperation and labour, for the purpose of promoting beneficial economic relations, based on principles to be agreed upon, as well as on human-development considerations on a regional basis …

c To cooperate bilaterally, as well as in multilateral forums, towards the promotion of their respective economies and of their neighbourly economic relations with other regional parties.

Beyond the confines of the palace, the continued support of prominent East Bank families for the Hashemite claim to rule Jordan is crucial to a smooth transition. Discontent over the country's precarious economic situation is therefore of particular concern. Jordan is burdened by a substantial debt of approximately $6bn – in part due to the need to maintain a substantial bureaucracy to ensure

East Bankers' employment – and high unemployment rates of 15% (unofficial rates are 25%).[39] Frustration led to riots in 1989 and 1996, sparked by price rises for basic foodstuffs.

Disaffection with the economy is compounded by the failure of the 1994 Jordan–Israel Peace Treaty to deliver its promised peace dividend.[40] The significant economic cooperation between Israel and Jordan envisaged by the treaty has failed to appear, partly because Israel has been less than forthcoming in joint projects and in facilitating Jordanian exports to West Bank Palestinian markets. Thousands of Jordanians are employed in Jordan's Qualifying Industrial Zone, in the Irbid industrial estate, which offers duty-free status in US markets to goods jointly produced by Israelis and Jordanians.[41] Even so, critics accuse the Israelis of temporising over projects intended for the Zone. Meetings of the Jordanian–Israeli trade committee have suffered from postponements and setbacks, primarily due to the failure to reach agreement on Jordanian exports to Israel.[42] There have also been problems in implementing joint Israeli–Jordanian operation of Aqaba airport.[43] In early 1998, reports emerged that Israel was planning to close its trade office in Jordan due to lack of activity; although the office remained open, the possibility of its closure caused uproar.

Material disappointment exacerbates ideological opposition to the peace treaty among the country's Islamists, nationalists and leftists. The erratic progress of the Palestinian–Israeli peace process means that King Hussein is left with precisely the type of unilateral peace that he long sought to avoid. Popular suspicion of the treaty is expressed in *peace with Israel fuels discontent* concerns that Jordan is compromising the pan-Arab cause in favour of relations with Israel and the West.[44] Jordan's acquiescence in US policy towards Iraq, together with the Jordanian military's observer status in US–Turkey–Israel naval exercises in January 1998, reinforce this sense of betrayal.

The peace treaty has strained relations between the MB and the regime. The MB strongly opposes normalisation with Israel, including those economic measures that might make peace viable in the long term. In late 1997, the IAF launched a campaign calling for the reversal of a law passed earlier in the year designed to attract foreign investment by allowing 100% foreign (including Israeli) ownership of banking, telecommunications, transport and insurance companies.[45] The Islamist boycott of the 1997 parliamentary elections, which succeeded in keeping voters away from the polls, was prompted in part by a May 1997 amendment to the press and publications law intended to marginalise the treaty's opponents.[46] For Leith Shubeilat, the head of the powerful MB-dominated engineers' association and long-time critic of the regime, 'Jordan not only has signed a peace treaty with Israel but has become a tail to the [Israelis] and the imperialists (Americans) and we oppose that'.[47] Shubeilat was arrested for inciting demonstrations in Amman, Irbid and Ma'an – a traditional tribal stronghold – in February 1998.

Securing the Hashemite monarchy depends on the steadfast commitment of the East Bank tribes to the regime. King Hussein has traditionally relied on foreign aid and support to accomplish this. From the mid-1970s, aid came principally from the Gulf countries, but King Hussein's backing for Saddam in 1991 foreclosed this support. Peace with Israel – with its promise of foreign aid, tourism, joint development projects and an influx of foreign investment – is therefore crucial as a basis for sustained economic development. King Hussein has withstood ideological criticism and has been forced to shelve democratic reforms to stave off opposition in the hope that, in the long term, peace with Israel and the broader alliance with the US will ensure regime security.[48]

Against the backdrop of social discontent, the military's apparent support for the Hashemites offers reassurance that the succession will be smooth. At the same time, however, maintaining this support will cause a subtle shift in the regime's political–military balance. Hussein's use of repression since the mid-1990s – a restrictive press law, a less representative electoral law, and the adoption of more intrusive internal-security measures – has increased the regime's reliance on the military and security forces. Hassan's lack of military credentials is, as one Jordanian journalist put it, 'extremely significant' given this greater dependence. In the event of growing social turmoil and demonstrations, similar to those in Ma'an in February 1998, King Hussein's son Abdullah could be decisive in helping his uncle to retain power. Born in 1962, Abdullah is widely popular in the military, and is head of the important Special Operations Command, which includes the Royal Guard.

Abdullah's military credentials are important in part because of Hassan's lack of a formal military background. According to a Jordanian journalist:

> *Abdullah sleeps, eats and trains with the military; he speaks their language, whereas Hassan is an intellectual and has trouble establishing a rapport with the military ... when he wears a uniform he looks out of place.*[49]

Hassan will have to rely on his senior commanders until he builds support within the regime's core constituencies, and within the military establishment at large. To accomplish the former, Hassan may be prompted to accommodate opposition to Jordan's treaty with Israel in a way that his older brother has heretofore avoided.

Especially in the months leading up to the treaty and subsequently, King Hussein has back-tracked on efforts to make the regime more resilient in his absence by increasing the power of parliamentary institutions and encouraging the growth of ideological parties at the expense of tribal ties. Despite the King's reputed interest in expanding the role of parliament and party competition, there are dangers in doing so. The opposition, especially Islamists and leftists and their respective political parties, are ardently opposed to some of the King's policies, especially his peace treaty with Israel and acquiescence in US policy towards Iraq. Hence, in the process of securing the Hashemites through liberalisation, he could prompt the steady erosion of their influence, as well as undermine his pro-Western 'grand strategy'.

Regional Implications

Leadership succession in Syria, Egypt and Jordan will fundamentally affect the domestic politics of these states. But its impact will also be felt outside them. Historically, internal change in one country in the Middle East has fundamentally altered the strategic interaction among the region's states. In particular, Jordan's geostrategic importance makes its stability crucial. Situated between Israel, Syria, Iraq and Saudi Arabia, Jordan is a vital buffer zone. All these countries, as well as the US and European states, have a stake in a smooth succession there. In Syria, prolonged instability could lead to unpredictable military and security policies, as competing groups vie for influence or a new leader seeks to consolidate his grip on power. The militancy of Assad's rhetoric and support for radical forces in the region notwithstanding, the Assad regime pursues a relatively pragmatic foreign policy. A more ambitious approach by a less secure successor could have serious regional implications.

The nature of the post-succession regimes in Syria and Jordan will have important implications for Arab–Israeli peace. A greater voice for the opposition in Jordan, for example, could jeopardise the country's controversial peace treaty. Even without profound change, a less secure leader in Amman may be less able to manage peace, while a weaker leader in Syria may find it more difficult to achieve.

The possibility of civil war in Syria, Iraq or Jordan, between or among minority interests and the countries' largely disenfranchised majorities, also cannot be discounted. Civil conflict could raise the prospect of significant refugee flows, an endemic regional problem, and could ignite simmering ethnic and religious tensions within other states. Thus, despite the widespread antipathy towards Saddam's regime in Iraq, considerable apprehension surrounds efforts to press for his removal. Finally, the fact that so many Middle Eastern regimes face uncertain transitions raises the sobering prospect of profound instability and change in this strategically vital region.

conclusion

Once noted for its coups and counter-coups, the Arab world has witnessed remarkable leadership stability since the 1970s. In Egypt, political control is maintained largely through providing the military with private and corporate benefits; institutional checks, such as rotating commands, are also useful instruments. In Jordan, tribal relations underpin political control. Traditionally, Transjordanians have not only been the main beneficiaries of political power, but have also occupied the key positions in the armed forces. The interests of the military therefore overlap with those of the regime, lessening the need for punitive control measures such as purges. Beyond his tribal bedrock, King Hussein's personal popularity and delicate management of Palestinian affairs, if not of relations with the PLO, have strengthened the monarchy and reduced its explicit reliance on force. Assad has built his regime on the Alawi minority, while the vast security apparatus limits the spread of sectarian, class, ideological or other grievances in the military. Assad has also been sensitive to the need to court the Sunni majority and maintain his support in the *Ba'ath* Party, as well as overseeing the expansion of commercial interests stimulated by economic reform. Finally, Saddam has established multiple security agencies designed to prevent conspiracies against his regime. Regular rotations and purges ensure that few officers are in place long enough to contemplate, let alone organise, a coup, while the severe punishments meted out to suspected plotters are a further disincentive to rebellion. At the same time, Saddam has tried to expand his tribal network and maintain the *Ba'ath* Party as a pillar of support for the regime.

The fact that regimes have successfully managed political–military relations does not necessarily imply that the military's importance has diminished. The armed forces remain powerful behind-the-scenes constituencies, whose support must be maintained and opposition guarded against. There is therefore an inherent tension between preserving domestic stability and encouraging dramatic economic and political reform.

Limited economic liberalisation is possible under existing conditions, and is proceeding to varying degrees in Egypt, Syria and Jordan. However, comprehensive market reform is potentially destabilising, especially where it threatens military prerogatives by, for example, causing weapons acquisition to decline, reducing officers' perquisites and/or standards of living, privatising the military's economic activities, establishing legislative accountability or requiring transparency in military activities. Similarly, political liberalisation – and democratisation – can only proceed so far before challenging the military's institutional and financial prerogatives. Hence, short-term stability is bought at the expense of the long-term political and economic transformation of these regimes.

the prospects for reform are limited by the military

Political–military relations will be crucial in the impending leadership successions in key Arab states. The uncertainties surrounding succession offer opportunities for profound leadership change. Leadership stability cannot be taken for granted, even where designated successors exist. A comprehensive assessment of the challenges that new leaders will face must take account of the various aspects of political control, and must not assume that military support will be forthcoming.

Outside states can participate in these processes, and can assist new leaders in securing their positions. International support and resources help both to bolster popular backing for new leaders, and to service vital constituencies, including the military. By helping to satisfy the corporate interests of the armed forces, military aid can ease the task of consolidating power. Finally, foreign military assistance, joint training and military education can assist in building important ties with senior officers, and create vested interests within the officer corps.

Ultimately, the inevitable leadership successions facing key Arab states may take place smoothly, with only minor implications for the complexion of these regimes. However, the Free Officers 'revolution' in Egypt in the 1950s, the ousting of the Hashemite monarchy in Iraq in 1958, and the birth of Iran as an Islamic Republic in 1979 all fundamentally altered relations between the states of the region and beyond.

The strategies regimes have used in the 1990s are essential for securing political control over the military, and underpin the stability of contemporary Arab regimes. But maintaining this control is a continuous and evolving process, and past success does not guarantee future stability. A breakdown in social support for the leadership, failure to detect a conspiracy within the military and economic or political change that threatens military prerogatives could all disrupt the equilibrium in political–military relations. Complacency about current stability leaves outsiders unprepared for the real prospect of change.

Extracts from the Constitutions of Egypt, Jordan and Syria

Egypt
Article 75
The President of the Republic should be an Egyptian born to Egyptian parents and enjoy civil and political rights. His age must not be less than 40 Gregorian years.

Article 76
The People's Assembly shall nominate the President of the Republic. The nomination shall be referred to the people for a plebiscite. The nomination for the President of the Republic shall be made in the People's Assembly upon the proposal of at least one third of its members. The candidate who obtains two thirds of the votes of the members of the People's Assembly shall be referred to the people for a plebiscite. If he does not obtain the said majority the nomination process shall be repeated two days after the first vote. The candidate obtaining an absolute majority of the votes of the Assembly members shall be referred to the citizens for a plebiscite. The candidate shall be considered President of the Republic when he obtains an absolute majority of votes cast in the plebiscite. If the candidate does not obtain this majority, the Assembly shall propose the nomination of another candidate and the same procedure shall follow concerning his candidature and election.

Article 82

In case the President of the Republic, due to any temporary obstacle, is unable to carry out his functions, he shall delegate his powers to a Vice-President.

Article 84

In case of the vacancy of the Presidential office or the permanent disability of the President of the Republic, the Speaker of the People's Assembly shall temporarily assume the Presidency. In case the People's Assembly is dissolved at such a time the President of the Supreme Constitutional Court shall take over the Presidency on condition that neither one shall nominate himself for the Presidency.

Jordan
Article 28

The Throne of the Hashemite Kingdom of Jordan is hereditary to the dynasty of King Abdullah Ibn Al-Hussein in a direct line through his male heirs as provided hereinafter:

> (a) The Royal title shall pass from the holder of the Throne to his eldest son, and to the eldest son of that son and in linear succession by a similar process thereafter. Should the eldest son die before the Throne devolves upon him, his eldest son shall inherit the Throne despite the existence of brothers to the deceased son. The King may, however, select one of his brothers as heir apparent. In this event, title to the Throne shall pass to him from the holder of the Throne.

> (b) Should the person entitled to the Throne die without a male heir, the Throne shall pass to his eldest brother. In the event that the holder of the Throne has no brothers, the Throne shall pass to the eldest son of his eldest brother. Should his eldest brother have no son, the Throne shall pass to the eldest son of his other brothers according to their seniority in age.

(c) In the absence of any brothers or nephews, the Throne shall pass to the uncles and their descendants, according to the order prescribed in paragraph (b) above.

(d) Should the last King die without any heir in the manner prescribed above, the Throne shall devolve upon the person whom the National Assembly shall select from amongst the descendants of the founder of the Arab Revolt, the late King Hussein Ibn Ali.

(e) No person shall ascend the Throne unless he is a Moslem, mentally sound and born by a legitimate wife and of Moslem parents.

(f) No person shall ascend the Throne who has been excluded from succession by a Royal Decree on the ground of unsuitability. Such exclusion shall not of itself include the descendants of such person. The Royal Decree of exclusion shall be countersigned by the Prime Minister and by four Ministers, at least two of whom shall be the Minister of Interior and the Minister of Justice.

(g) The King attains his majority upon the completion of his eighteenth year according to the lunar calendar. If the Throne devolves upon a person who is below this age, the powers of the King shall be exercised by a Regent or Council of Regency ...

(h) Should the King become unable to exercise his powers on account of illness, his powers shall be exercised by a vicegerent or Council of Vicegerents ...

Syria
Article 83
A candidate for the presidency must be an Arab Syrian, enjoying his civil and political rights, and be over 40 years of age.

Article 84

Upon the proposal of the Arab Socialist *Ba'ath* Party regional command, the Assembly issues the order for election of the President:

> 1) the candidacy is proposed to the citizens for referendum;
> 2) the referendum takes place upon the request of the President of the Assembly;
> 3) the new President is elected before termination of the term of the present President, within a period of not less than 30 days and not more than 60 days;
> 4) the candidate becomes President of the Republic if he obtains an absolute majority of the total votes ...

Article 88

The first Vice President of the Republic or the Vice President named by the President carries out the President's duties if the President fails to do so. If the incapacity is permanent or in case of death or resignation, a referendum takes place to elect a new President in accordance with the provisions of Article 84 ...

Article 89

If the post of President becomes vacant and there is no Vice President, the Prime Minister exercises all the President's powers and jurisdictions until a new President is elected by means of referendum within 90 days.

Definitions

This paper uses the term 'military' to refer to the high command and the senior officer corps – those in charge of the military establishment on a day-to-day basis. Political leaders are those in charge of the state's broad policy concerns, regardless of whether they came to power through a coup or are former military officers. The 'military establishment' refers to all the service branches, units and forces that comprise them.

Sources

Much of the research for this paper involved interviews with officials and analysts in Amman, Cairo and Tel Aviv (June 1998); Washington DC (March 1998); and London (between October 1997 and June 1998). Because of the topic's sensitivity, in many cases names and titles have been omitted from citations.

Introduction

[1] According to Ekkart Zimmerman, 40 coup attempts involving 11 countries took place between 1958 and 1973. See Zimmerman, 'Toward a Causal Model of Military Coups d'Etat', *Armed Forces and Society*, vol. 5, no. 3, Spring 1979, pp. 387–413. Also see Eliezer Be'eri, 'The Waning of the Military Coup in Arab Politics', *Middle Eastern Studies*, vol. 18, no. 1, January 1982, p. 69.
[2] Notable exceptions include Elizabeth Picard, 'Arab Military in Politics: From Revolutionary Plot to Authoritarian State', in Giacomo Luciano, *The Arab State* (Berkeley, CA: University of California Press, 1990), pp. 189–219; and Nazih Ayubi, *Over-stating the Arab State* (London: I. B. Tauris, 1995), especially chapter 8.
[3] Although this study focuses on the Arab world, its implications are not exclusive to the Middle East. In all authoritarian regimes, leaders face the dilemma of relying on their militaries to retain office,

while at the same time protecting themselves from military challenges. Former Indonesian President Suharto, who became head of state in 1967, used institutional safeguards – selective appointments, posting rotations and divide-and-rule tactics – to control the armed forces. When economic turbulence prompted mass social opposition, however, the military moved to oust Suharto in May 1998. Chile also demonstrates the importance of cultivating social support in shaping political–military relations. The enduring popularity of the armed forces has stymied civilian efforts to reclaim military prerogatives, including the crucial right to dismiss military commanders. Turkey illustrates the implications of challenging the military's corporate interests. The strongly secular armed forces resent the pro-Islamist agenda of some Turkish political parties because it impinges on these interests; in June 1997, the military forced the Islamist *Refah* (Welfare) party from office for these reasons. In the future, growing social support for pro-Islamist political leaders and the military's antipathy towards them will be a source of friction in political–military relations.

Chapter 1

[1] Iraq attained formal independence from the UK in 1932, and, four years later, became the first post-colonial Arab state to succumb to a military coup.
[2] Be'eri, 'The Waning of the Military Coup in Arab Politics', p. 69.

[3] 'Native East Bank Jordanians' refers to the descendants of the Bedouin tribes that were early inhabitants of the area. 'Non-native' refers to Palestinians who emigrated to the area after the Palestine War of 1948 and the Arab–Israeli War of 1967.
[4] For an excellent account of these events, see Patrick Seale, *Asad: The Struggle for the Middle East* (Berkeley, CA: University of California Press, 1988), p. 333.
[5] See Nikolaos Van Dam, *The Struggle for Power in Syria: Politics and Society under Asad and the Ba'ath Party*, Third Edition (London: I. B. Tauris, 1996), pp. 119–20.
[6] Be'eri, 'The Waning of the Military Coup in Arab Politics', p. 80.
[7] See, for example, Steve Negus, 'The Press Goes Too Far', *Middle East International*, 24 October 1997, pp. 10–11; John Lancaster, 'In Egypt, Testing Press Freedoms Can Provoke Official Backlash', *Washington Post*, 8 October 1997, p. A27; and Steve Negus, 'Mubarak's Press Dilemma', *Middle East International*, 13 March 1998, pp. 14–15.
[8] See, for example, *Amnesty International Report 1998* (London: Amnesty International Publications, 1998), pp. 322–33; and *Freedom in the World, 1995–1996* (New York: Freedom House, 1996), pp. 443–45.
[9] Cassandra, 'The Impending Crisis in Egypt', *Middle East Journal*, vol. 49, no. 1, Winter 1995, pp. 9–27.
[10] See 'Chief of Staff, Other Officials Inspect Military Units in Ma'an', Jordanian television report, in *BBC Summary of World Broadcasts, The Middle East* (SWB/ME) 3160, 25 February 1998, p. 20.

Chapter 2

[1] The literature on political–military relations is extensive. Examples include Samuel Finer, *The Man on Horseback: The Role of the Military in Politics* (Boulder, CO: Westview Press, 1988); and Roman Kolkowicz and Andrzej Korbonski (eds), *Soldiers, Peasants and Bureaucrats* (London: George Allen and Unwin, 1982). On how civilians politicise the military to control it, see Samuel P. Huntington, *The Soldier and the State* (Harvard, MA: Belknap, 1957).

[2] Adeed Dawisha notes that, in the case of Syria, 'the primary weakness in the military's power-relationship with the presidency relate[s] to Asad's popularity and prestige domestically, and his … stature internationally'. The same description applies equally to Egypt and Jordan. See Dawisha, 'Syria under Assad, 1970–78: The Centres of Power', *Government and Opposition*, vol. 13, no. 3, Summer 1978, p. 352.

[3] On the tactical complexities of staging a coup, see Edward Luttwak, *Coup D'Etat* (Cambridge, MA: Harvard University Press, 1980); and Bruce Farcau, *The Coup: Tactics in the Seizure of Power* (Westport, CT: Praeger, 1994).

[4] Volker Perthes, 'Stages of Economic and Political Liberalization', in Eberhard Kienle (ed.), *Contemporary Syria: Liberalization between Cold War and Cold Peace* (London: I. B. Tauris, 1994), p. 45.

[5] Alasdair Drysdale and Raymond A. Hinnebush, *Syria and the Middle East Peace Process* (New York: Council on Foreign Relations, 1991), p. 23.

[6] The Alawi minority is sometimes identified as a strand of the Shi'i branch of Islam.

[7] For details of the Alawi dominance of the *Ba'ath* Party, see Van Dam, *The Struggle for Power in Syria*, pp. 125–29.

[8] Eyal Zisser, *Decision-Making in Asad's Syria*, Washington Institute Policy Memorandum 35 (Washington DC: Washington Institute for Near East Policy, February 1998), pp. 10–11.

[9] *Ibid.*, p. 13.

[10] See, for example, Mariam Shahin, 'Secret to the Economic Future', *The Middle East*, February 1995, pp. 27–29; 'Not So Neighbourly', *ibid.*, February 1998, pp. 14–16; and Alan George, 'Businessmen by Nature', *ibid.*, November 1993, pp. 28–29. For a less optimistic view of the regime's economic reforms, see 'Leisurely Reform Stifles Innovation', *Middle East Economic Digest*, 29 September 1995, p. 10.

[11] The growing influence of commercial interests is evident in the expanded role of Chambers of Commerce in economic policy-making, the rejuvenation of the People's Assembly and the appointment to sensitive positions in the regime of individuals with experience of managing civilian agencies. See Fred Lawson, 'Private Capital and the State in Contemporary Syria', *Middle East Report*, Spring 1997, pp. 9, 11.

[12] Perthes, 'Stages of Economic and Political Liberalization', p. 68.

[13] See Patrick Seale, 'Preface', in Kienle (ed.), *Contemporary Syria*, p. xii. On the potential for antagonism, see Lawson, 'Private Capital', p. 13.

[14] *Infitah*, a common term in the Arab world, refers to policies that

'increase the weight of the private sector, open economies up internationally, involve a greater reliance on market forces and may include public sector reforms'. Perthes, 'Stages of Economic and Political Liberalization', p. 45.

[15] Ayubi, *Over-stating the Arab State*, p. 299.

[16] Between 1976 and 1980–81, expenditure on the security apparatus and armed forces grew by 139.6% at fixed prices. In the same period, education spending stagnated, and health-care spending declined. See Ayubi, *Over-stating the Arab State*, p. 301.

[17] Nazih Ayubi, 'Domestic Politics', in Lillian Craig Harris (ed.), *Egypt: Internal Challenges and Regional Stability*, Chatham House Paper 39 (London: Routledge for the Royal Institute of International Affairs, 1988), pp. 49–78.

[18] For a commentary and survey of Egypt's economy and its economic-reform programme, see David Batter, 'Special Report: Egypt', *Middle East Economic Digest*, vol. 42, no. 16, 17 April 1998, pp. 25–45.

[19] Despite economic reform, by mid-1997 only 120,000 public-sector jobs had been shed. See *Civil Society*, Ibn Khaldoun Center Newsletter, vol. 7, no. 74, February 1998, p. 15; and Mark Huband, '"Pre-democratic" Struggles', *Financial Times*, 13 May 1997, p. 3.

[20] See Robert Springborg, *Mubarak's Egypt: Fragmentation of the Political Order* (Boulder, CO: Westview Press, 1989), especially pp. 104–18.

[21] According to a British military officer with access to this information, there are signs of discontent among the officer corps at the wealth and privileges enjoyed by Egypt's new middle class. Personal communication, Cairo, June 1998.

[22] 'Back in High Gear', *Middle East Monitor*, vol. 8, no. 5, May 1998, p. 9.

[23] The regime is trying to channel investment to Upper Egypt, where Islamist militants have traditionally operated, in a bid to reduce their appeal. See *Civil Society*, p. 17. Also see Batter, 'Special Report', p. 26.

[24] See Huband, '"Pre-democratic" Struggles'.

[25] Laurie A. Brand, *Jordan's Inter-Arab Relations: The Political Economy of Alliance Making* (New York: Columbia University Press, 1994), p. 73.

[26] *Ibid.*, p. 49.

[27] Ibrahim A. Karawan, *The Islamist Impasse*, Adelphi Paper 314 (Oxford: Oxford University Press for the IISS, 1997), p. 23.

[28] Personal communication, US analyst of the Egyptian military, Washington DC, March 1998.

[29] Ofra Bengio, 'Iraq', in Ami Ayalon (ed.), *Middle East Contemporary Survey, Volume 13* (Boulder, CO: Westview Press, 1991), pp. 387–88.

[30] Michael Eisenstadt, *Like a Phoenix from the Ashes?: The Future of Iraqi Military Power*, Washington Institute Policy Paper 36 (Washington DC: Washington Institute for Near East Policy, 1993), p. 61.

[31] Crackdowns on opium-growing in the Bekaa Valley resulted in Syria's removal in November 1997 from the US list of countries suspected of producing or shipping illegal drugs. Donald Neff, 'No More Heroin in the Beqaa', *Middle East International*, 5 December 1997, p. 14.

[32] See 'Drug Cultivation and

Trafficking in Lebanon', in *Syria Unmasked: The Suppression of Human Rights by the Asad Regime* (New Haven, CT: Yale University Press for Middle East Watch, 1991), Appendix F; and James Bruce, 'Changes in the Syrian High Command', *Jane's Intelligence Review*, vol. 7, no. 3, March 1995, p. 127.

[33] *Syria Unmasked*, p. 164.

[34] See 'Syria Cracks Down on Smugglers', *Middle East International*, 23 July 1993, p. 19.

[35] *The Military Balance 1998/99* (Oxford: Oxford University Press for the IISS, 1998), p. 272.

[36] Personal communication, US military analyst, Washington DC, March 1998.

[37] See 'Syria Cracks Down on Smugglers'.

[38] See Springborg, *Mubarak's Egypt*, pp. 104–18.

[39] Cassandra, 'The Impending Crisis in Egypt', p. 23.

[40] Springborg, *Mubarak's Egypt*, pp. 104–107.

[41] Ahmed Abdalla, 'The Armed Forces and the Democratic Process in Egypt', *Third World Quarterly*, vol. 10, no. 4, October 1998, pp. 1,452–66.

[42] Yezid Sayigh, *Arab Military Industry* (London: Brassey's, 1992), pp. 45, 55–59.

[43] US officials visiting Egypt's arms-production plants regularly report concerns about operating standards. Personal communication, London, March 1998.

[44] In discussions about the M1 project in the 1980s, then Egyptian Defence Minister Abdel al-Halim Abu Ghazala expressed confidence that the tank could not only 'be produced at a commercially viable unit price (compared with American prices), but at even lower cost than in the USA owing to mainly lower labour costs'. The Americans insisted that each tank would cost \$4 million in total (initial investment for the plant, tooling, training, development and production), compared with \$3m per unit when imported into Egypt under Foreign Military Supply (FMS) and \$2m per unit when supplied to the US army. According to US officials, Egyptian-produced tanks have proved more expensive than their US-made counterparts. See Sayigh, *Arab Military Industry*, p. 81; interviews with US Office of Management and Budget (OMB) officials, Washington DC, March 1998; and Robert Lowry, 'Military Still Looks to West for Doctrine', *Jane's Defence Weekly*, 28 February 1996, p. 22.

[45] Springborg, *Mubarak's Egypt*, p. 109; and 'Egypt: Mubarak Hits Army Base', *Middle East Economic Digest*, 28 April 1989, p. 7.

[46] *The Military Balance 1998/99*, p. 272.

[47] Interviews with US OMB personnel and congressional appropriations committee staff, Washington DC, March 1998.

[48] Cassandra, 'The Impending Crisis in Egypt', p. 22.

[49] *Ibid.*, p. 23.

[50] Ed Blanche, 'Walking a Tightrope with the Hashemites', *Jane's Defence Weekly*, 15 January 1997, p. 17.

[51] *Ibid.*, p. 17.

[52] See, for example, Scott Peterson, 'Key Peace Player Jordan Feels Slighted by US', *Christian Science Monitor*, 20 October 1997.

[53] Discussion with senior British military officer stationed in the region, June 1998.

54 US Department of State, *Congressional Presentation for Foreign Operations, Fiscal Year 1997* (Washington DC: US Government Printing Office (GPO), 1996), p. 426.

55 See Eisenstadt, *Like a Phoenix from the Ashes?*, pp. 7–8.

56 See Hanna Batatu, 'Some Observations on the Social Roots of Syria's Ruling Military Group and the Cause for its Dominance', *Middle East Journal*, vol. 35, no. 3, Summer 1981, pp. 331–34. The current figure is given in Zisser, *Decision-Making in Asad's Syria*, p. 13.

57 See Zisser, *Decision-Making in Asad's Syria*, p. 15; and *Syria Unmasked*, chapter 4.

58 Drysdale and Hinnebush, *Syria and the Middle East Peace Process*, p. 29.

59 Iraq's ethnic divisions overlay its religious ones: the country's Arab population represents between 75% and 80% of the total, with ethnic Kurds, Turkomans and Assyrians making up the remainder.

60 See Anthony H. Cordesman and Ahmed S. Hashim, *Iraq: Sanctions and Beyond* (Boulder, CO: Westview Press, 1997), p. 12.

61 On purges and rotations in the war's aftermath, see Michael Eisenstadt, 'The Iraqi Armed Forces Two Years On', *Jane's Intelligence Review*, March 1993, pp. 121–26.

62 Samuel M. Katz, 'Still Partners', *The Jerusalem Report*, 27 November 1997, pp. 18–19.

63 Van Dam, *The Struggle for Power in Syria*, p. 124.

64 Amatzia Baram, 'Neo-Tribalism in Iraq: Saddam Hussein's Tribal Policies 1991–96', *International Journal of Middle East Studies*, vol. 29, no. 1, February 1997, pp. 1–31; and Cordesman and Hashim, *Iraq*, pp. 12–13.

65 See Baram, 'Neo-Tribalism in Iraq', pp. 7–18.

66 See, for example, 'Tribes Enter Palace, Pledge Loyalty to Saddam', *Al-Thawrah*, 19 November 1997, in SWB/ME D3085, 25 November 1997, p. 6; and Baram, 'Neo-Tribalism in Iraq', p. 13.

67 Baram, 'Neo-Tribalism in Iraq', p. 20.

68 See Doug Struck, 'In Southern Iraq, the '91 Revolt is Long Over', *International Herald Tribune*, 22 April 1998, p. 4.

69 See, for example, John Lancaster and David B. Ottaway, 'Saddam Curbs Role of Kin in Iraq's Regime', *Washington Post*, 22 October 1995, p. AO1.

70 *Keesing's Contemporary Archives*, February 1995, p. 40,622.

71 See Van Dam, *The Struggle for Power in Syria*, chapter 6.

72 Field Marshal Abdel Hakim Amer's removal is part of a long line of politically motivated dismissals from the military. Other casualties of this process include Minister of War and Chief of Staff Mohammed Fawzi (1971); Minister of War Mohammad Sadiq (1972); Chief of Staff Saad al-Din Shazli (1973); Minister of Defence General Abdel al-Ghani Gamasi and Chief of Staff Mohammad Ali Fahmi (1978); and Minister of Defence Abu Ghazala (1989). See Springborg, *Mubarak's Egypt*, p. 97.

73 John Keegan, *World Armies* (London: Macmillan, 1979), p. 204.

74 *Syria Unmasked*, p. 9. See Keegan, *World Armies* (1983 edition), p. 695.

75 John Kifner, 'Syrian Troops Are Said to Battle Rebels Encircled in Central City', *New York Times*, 12 February 1982, p. 1; and 'Syrian

Chief Is Said to Thwart Planned Coup', *ibid.*, 6 February 1982, p. 6.

[76] Although Jordan's Royal Guard has traditionally been outside the army's command structure, in 1996 it was merged with the Special Forces Brigade under the newly formed Royal Jordanian Special Operations Command. See Katz, 'Still Partners', p. 18.

[77] See Zisser, *Decision-Making in Asad's Syria*; and *Syria Unmasked*, pp. 38–53.

[78] See, for example, Carl Anthony Wege, 'Assad's Legions: The Syrian Intelligence Services', *Intelligence and Counterintelligence*, vol. 4, no. 1, Spring 1990, p. 97; and *Syria Unmasked*, pp. 42–43.

[79] See Sean Boyne, 'Inside Iraq's Security Network, Part One', *Jane's Intelligence Review*, July 1997, pp. 312–14; and Andrew Rathmell, 'Iraqi Intelligence and Security Services', *International Defence Review*, vol. 24, no. 5, May 1991, p. 393.

[80] Iraqi General Intelligence developed from the *Jihaz Haneen*, the *Ba'ath* Party security organisation set up by Saddam Hussein in the mid-1960s and used to great effect in his rise to power. The Military Security Service, formerly part of Military Intelligence, was made into its own agency in 1992. See Boyne, 'Inside Iraq's Security Network', pp. 313, 366–77.

[81] Lancaster and Ottaway, 'Saddam Curbs Role of Kin'.

[82] Personal communication with US analyst of the Egyptian military, Washington DC, March 1998; and with British military officer, Cairo, June 1998.

[83] In conventional usage, 'professionalisation' in the Egyptian army commonly refers to the use of merit-based standards in appointments, attention to duty and mission and reluctance to become involved in domestic political conflicts. On the general concept of professionalism, see Huntington, *The Soldier and the State*, especially pp. 7–19.

[84] See Lowry, 'Military Still Looks to West for Doctrine', p. 21; 'Back in High Gear', p. 9; 'A Revolution to End the Revolution', *The Economist*, 25 October 1997, p. 87; and personal communication, Washington DC, March 1998.

[85] Committee Against Repression and for Democratic Rights (CARDRI), *Saddam's Iraq: Revolution or Reaction?* (London: Zed Books, 1989), p. 222.

[86] See Cordesman and Hashim, *Iraq*, p. 50.

[87] Eisenstadt, 'The Iraqi Armed Forces Two Years On', pp. 122–23.

[88] In Egypt, Chief of Staff Lieutenant-General Salah Halabi, who was replaced by General Magdi Hatata in October 1995, is thought to have been a casualty of this rotation process. See James Bruce, 'Country Briefing: Egypt', *Jane's Defence Weekly*, 28 February 1996, p. 22.

[89] Van Dam, *The Struggle for Power in Syria*, p. 118.

[90] See Bruce, 'Changes in the Syrian High Command'.

[91] *The Military Balance, 1998/99*, p. 131.

[92] By 1990, Syria owed the Soviet Union and East European countries an estimated $14–15 billion, half of which was probably for military equipment. See *The Military Balance, 1991–1992* (London: Brassey's for the IISS, 1991), p. 120.

[93] Anthony Cordesman, *Perilous Prospects: The Peace Process and the*

Arab–Israeli Military Balance
(Boulder, CO: Westview Press,
1996), p. 17.
[94] *The Military Balance, 1998/99,*
p. 125.

Chapter 3

[1] For a comprehensive analysis of
Arab military effectiveness, see
Kenneth M. Pollack, *The Arabs at
War: Arab Military Effectiveness from
1945 to 1991* (Ithaca, NY: Cornell
University Press, forthcoming).
[2] Interview with Western military
officer, Cairo, June 1998.
[3] Interviews with analysts and
officials, Washington DC, March
1998, and Cairo, June 1998. Also
see Drew Middleton, 'US Aides
Say Egypt Lacks Ability to Handle
Weapons', *New York Times*, 21
February 1986, p. 8.
[4] Steve Negus, 'Playing the US War
Games', *Middle East International*, 7
November 1997, p. 13.
[5] Pollack cites the concerns of
numerous US Department of
Defense officials about these
issues. He attributes many of these
problems to cultural, as well as
political, factors. On Egypt in the
Gulf War, see Pollack, *The Arabs at
War*, pp. 165–76.
[6] Interview with Egyptian
journalist, Cairo, June 1998.
[7] Negus, 'Playing the US War
Games'.
[8] Interview with Western military
officer, Cairo, June 1998.
[9] George G. Gawrych, 'The
Egyptian High Command in the
1973 War', *Armed Forces and Society*,
no. 13, Summer 1987, p. 545.
[10] Richard B. Parker, *The Politics of
Miscalculation in the Middle East*
(Bloomington, IN: Indiana
University Press, 1993). On the

effects of political–military
relations on Egyptian capabilities
in the 1967 and 1973 wars, see Risa
Brooks, 'The Domestic Origins and
International Effects of Political–
Military Institutions', PhD
dissertation, University of
California, San Diego, CA,
forthcoming.
[11] Efraim Karsh, *The Iran–Iraq War:
A Military Analysis*, Adelphi Paper
220 (London: IISS, 1987), p. 43.
[12] Anthony H. Cordesman and
Abraham R. Wagner, *Lessons of
Modern War, Volume 1: The Arab–
Israeli Conflicts, 1973–1989*
(Boulder, CO: Westview Press,
1990), p. 289.
[13] Michael Eisenstadt, *Arming for
Peace? Syria's Elusive Quest for
'Strategic Parity'*, Washington
Institute Policy Paper 31
(Washington DC: Washington
Institute for Near East Policy,
1992), p. 58.
[14] Cordesman and Wagner, *Lessons
of Modern War, Volume 1*, p. 290.
[15] On these disputes, see
Eisenstadt, *Arming for Peace?*, p. 61.
[16] Interview with Western military
officer, Cairo, June 1998.
[17] See Cassandra, 'The Impending
Crisis in Egypt', p. 25.
[18] *Ibid*.
[19] Anthony H. Cordesman and
Abraham R. Wagner, *The Lessons of
Modern War, Volume 2: The Iran–Iraq
War* (Boulder, CO: Westview Press,
1990), pp. 58–59.
[20] Saddam had 300 officers purged
and 15 generals shot by mid-1982
for incompetence and dereliction
of duty. *Ibid.*, p. 44.
[21] Karsh, *The Iran–Iraq War*, p. 43.
[22] CARDRI, *Saddam's Iraq*, p. 223;
and Mark Heller, 'Iraq's Army:
Military Weakness, Political
Utility', in Amatzia Baram and
Barry Rubin (eds), *Iraq's Road to*

War (New York: St Martin's Press, 1996), p. 45.

[23] See Michael Eisenstadt, 'Syria's Defense Companies: Profile of a Praetorian Unit', unpublished manuscript, 1989, p. 7. Also see Van Dam, *The Struggle for Power in Syria*, p. 122.

[24] Cordesman and Hashim, *Iraq*, p. 260; and Karsh, *The Iran–Iraq War*, p. 43.

[25] Cordesman and Hashim, *Iraq*, p. 260.

[26] See Ayubi, *Over-stating the Arab State*, pp. 270–71.

[27] Opposition concerns are detailed in Abdalla, 'The Armed Forces and the Democratic Process in Egypt', especially p. 1,462; also see Ayubi, *Over-stating the Arab State*, pp. 275–76; personal communication with military analyst, Washington DC, March 1998.

[28] Roger Owen, 'Arab Armies Today', unpublished manuscript, 1987, cited in Ayubi, *Over-stating the Arab State*, p. 275.

[29] Eisenstadt, *Arming for Peace?*, p. 58.

[30] Cordesman, *Perilous Prospects*, p. 181.

[31] Personal communication with analyst/researcher, Washington DC, March 1998.

[32] Interview, Washington DC, March 1998.

[33] Springborg, *Mubarak's Egypt*, pp. 118–23; and Abdalla, 'The Armed Forces and the Democratic Process in Egypt', pp. 1,460–61.

[34] Melvin A. Friedlander, *Sadat and Begin: The Domestic Politics of Peacemaking* (Boulder, CO: Westview Press, 1983).

[35] On these reforms, see Cordesman and Wagner, *The Lessons of Modern War, Volume 2*, pp. 52–63; Pollack, *The Arabs at War*, pp. 265–68; and 'Iraq's Army: The Lessons from the War with Iran', *The Economist*, 12 January 1991, p. 36.

[36] For example, Saddam formed a new presidential security unit, the Special Security Service (*Amn al-Khas*). Analysts also trace the origins of the Special Republican Guard to the reforms; the Guard subsequently assumed responsibility for garrisoning Baghdad from the Republican Guard. See Rathmell, 'Iraqi Intelligence and Security Services', p. 393; and Boyne, 'Inside Iraq's Security Network', p. 314.

[37] Cordesman and Hashim, *Iraq*, pp. 261–62.

[38] For a nuanced analysis of Arab militaries in different battlefield scenarios, see Cordesman, *Perilous Prospects*. Cordesman also discusses political factors and other problems in the developing world's militaries; see *ibid.*, pp. 87–99. Pollack, *The Arabs at War*, provides a systematic analysis of the effects of political factors in Arab militaries between 1948 and 1991.

Chapter 4

[1] Emad S. Mekay, 'The View from Damascus', *Jerusalem Report*, 20 March 1997, p. 22.

[2] 'Father Figure', *The Economist*, 7 January 1995, p. 45.

[3] Interview with Syria analyst, London, May 1998.

[4] This list draws on Eyal Zisser, 'The Succession Struggle in Syria', *Middle East Quarterly*, vol. 2, no. 2, September 1995, pp. 57–64; and Zisser, *Decision-Making in Asad's Syria*. See these sources for a more extensive list. Also see Alasdair Drysdale, 'The Succession

Question in Syria', *Middle East Journal*, vol. 39, no. 2, Spring 1985, pp. 246–57.

[5] See Zisser, 'The Succession Struggle in Syria', p. 62.

[6] See Van Dam, *The Struggle for Power in Syria*, pp. 130–31; and Zisser, 'The Succession Struggle in Syria'.

[7] For a discussion of these personnel changes, see Zisser, 'The Succession Struggle in Syria'. Also see *Middle East Economic Digest*, 4 November 1994, p. 35.

[8] Bruce, 'Changes in the Syrian High Command', p. 126.

[9] Eyal Zisser, 'Syria', in Ami Ayalon and Bruce Maddy Wietzman (eds), *Middle East Contemporary Survey, Volume 18* (Boulder, CO: Westview Press, 1994), p. 614.

[10] 'Intelligence Service Head Dismissed, Reports London-based Paper', *Al-Hayat*, SWB/ME 3271, 6 July 1998, p. 18; and 'Shihabi Replaced as Army Chief-of-Staff', *ibid.*

[11] See 'Rifaat's Removal Again Raises Succession Issue', *Middle East Reporter*, vol. 86, no. 983, 14 February 1998, pp. 9–10; and *Syria*, Economist Intelligence Unit (EIU), Second Quarter 1998, pp. 11–12.

[12] Personal communication, Washington DC, March 1998.

[13] 'Rifaat Sacking Prompts Economic Reform Hopes', *Middle East Economic Digest*, vol. 40, no. 2, 20 February 1998, p. 26; 'Rifaat Sacking Seen as Business Boost', *Middle East Monitor*, vol. 8, no. 3, March 1998, p. 12.

[14] This theory was suggested by a frequent visitor and close analyst of Syrian domestic politics. Efforts to mobilise a new commercial élite to balance the old security networks are the corollary to eliminating key individuals who pose a potential challenge. Interview, Washington DC, March 1998.

[15] Springborg, *Mubarak's Egypt*, pp. 101–103. The year after the riots, Abu Ghazala's photograph appeared in the press almost as frequently as did Mubarak's. *Ibid.*, p. 103.

[16] 'Egypt: Mubarak Hits Army Base'; Patrick E. Taylor, 'Mubarak Reassigns Key Deputy', *Washington Post*, 16 April 1989, p. A29. On other theories surrounding Abu Ghazala's removal, see Ami Ayalon, 'Egypt', in Ayalon (ed.), *Middle East Contemporary Survey, Volume 13*, pp. 300–301. The present analysis also benefited from discussion with an Egyptian researcher, London, May 1998.

[17] 'Mubarak Says No Coup Behind Removal of Defence Minister', *Reuters Library Report*, 19 April 1989.

[18] Interview with Egyptian researcher, London, May 1998.

[19] 'Government Aware of Investment Gap', *Middle East Monitor*, vol. 8, no. 6, June 1998, p. 10.

[20] Both views were expressed by Egyptian academics and researchers in discussions on the topic in Cairo, June 1998.

[21] Analysts are divided over the extent of factionalism in the Egyptian military. The homogenous nature of Egyptian society makes ethnic or sectarian cleavages unlikely. However, the existence of competing patronage networks in the military indicates that factionalism may be present; anecdotal evidence provided by Western military officers suggests that cronyism in the military is increasing. One Western officer

notes that, in joint decision-making fora, it is customary not to look to the most senior officer, but to the individual known to have Mubarak's personal support, to evaluate Egyptian positions. See Cassandra, 'The Impending Crisis in Egypt', p. 23; and interview with British military officer, Cairo, June 1998.

[22] Interview with senior British embassy official, Cairo, June 1998.

[23] 'President Opens Military Hospital in Arish', *Egyptian Gazette*, 12 June 1998. Many existing military hospitals are under-used.

[24] Interview with retired Egyptian security official, Cairo, June 1998.

[25] Personal communication, US State Department official, Washington DC, March 1998.

[26] 'Massacre Further Divides Splintered Islamic Movement', *Middle East Reporter*, 13 December 1997, pp. 14–15.

[27] 'Interior Minister Says Army Will Have No Role in Guarding Tourist Sites', *MENA*, in SWB/ME 03085, 25 November 1997, p. 24.

[28] The Egyptian government, for example, took significant notice of the February 1998 Ma'an riots in Jordan and ensuing repression, wary of the message for its own delicate balance. Personal communication, US State Department official, Washington DC, March 1998.

[29] For a particularly alarmist view, see Joseph Kechichian and Jeanne Nazimek, 'Challenges to the Military in Egypt', *Middle East Policy*, vol. 5, no. 3, September 1997, pp. 129–31.

[30] Samia Nakhoul, 'Egyptian Militants Aim to Infiltrate Armed Forces', *Reuters*, 23 August 1993.

[31] Observers have suggested that information available only to high-level officials was essential to the 1994 assassination of Major General Ra'uf Khayrat, a key officer in the State Security Investigative Services. See Cassandra, 'The Impending Crisis in Egypt', p. 24.

[32] See Robert Fisk, 'Algeria's Past May Be Egypt's Future', *The Independent*, 21 February 1994, p. 10; and Nakhoul, 'Egyptian Militants Aim to Infiltrate Armed Forces'.

[33] Cassandra, 'The Impending Crisis in Egypt', p. 22.

[34] Interview with Jordanian journalist, Amman, June 1998.

[35] See Sana Kamal, 'Hassan at the Helm', *Middle East International*, vol. 10, 21 August 1998, p. 11.

[36] See 'King Hussein's Illness Raises Questions about Jordan's Future', *Associated Press*, 8 September 1998.

[37] See 'King Hussein Says Prince Hassan Remains Successor', *Mideast Mirror*, vol. 7, no. 33, 17 February 1993.

[38] Asher Susser, 'Jordan', in Ayalon and Wietzman (eds), *Middle East Contemporary Survey, Volume 18*, p. 432.

[39] 'Trade Agreement with Israel', *Middle East Monitor*, vol. 7, no. 1, January 1997, p. 10.

[40] See Lamis Andani, 'Has Jordan Turned Its Back on Pan-Arabism', *Middle East International*, 24 April 1998, pp. 18–19.

[41] Israel and Jordan agreed to create the Qualifying Industrial Zone at Irbid on 16 November 1997 under the requirements of Section 9 of the United States–Israel Free Trade Area Implementation Act, 1985. See 'Agreement between the Hashemite Kingdom of Jordan and

Israel on Irbid Qualifying Industrial Zone', www.jedco.gov.jo/agreement.htm.

[42] 'Trade Agreement with Israel', pp. 10–11; and 'A Mixed Peace Dividend', *ibid.*, June 1996, p. 12.

[43] 'Jordanian Official Says Israel Obstructing Aqaba Airport Flights Agreement', SWB/ME 3164, 2 March 1998, p. 13.

[44] See Androni, 'Has Jordan Turned Its Back', pp. 18–19.

[45] See 'Non-Violent Plan to Abrogate Peace Treaty', *Middle East Reporter*, vol. 85, no. 973, 22 November 1997.

[46] See 'Tribal Alliance Surmounts Ideologies', *Middle East Reporter*, vol. 85, no. 968, 18 October 1997, p. 7; and 'Amman Moves to Muzzle Critics of Peace Treaty with Israel', *Mideast Mirror*, vol. 9, no. 101, 30 May 1995, pp. 10–11. See also Alan Cowell, 'Jordan–Israel Ties: "Severe Wounds"', *International Herald Tribune*, 16 October 1997, p. 1; and 'Elections Expose Old Divisions', *Middle East Monitor*, vol. 7, no. 12, December 1997, pp. 12–13.

[47] 'King Hussein: Damned If He Does, Damned If He Doesn't', *Middle East Reporter*, 21 February 1998, p. 11.

[48] Interview with Jordanian journalist, Amman, June 1998.

[49] *Ibid.*